Bouldering with
Bobbi Bensman

Bouldering
with
Bobbi Bensman

Bobbi Bensman

STACKPOLE
BOOKS

To my grandfather, Jerome Moss.
May he always know how dear he is to my heart.
May he rest in peace.

Copyright © 1999 by Stackpole Books

Published by
STACKPOLE BOOKS
5067 Ritter Road
Mechanicsburg, PA 17055
www.stackpolebooks.com

Printed in the United States of America

10 9 8 7 6 5 4 3 2 1

First edition

Photographs by Jim Surette

Library of Congress Cataloging-in-Publication Data

Bensman, Bobbi.
    Bouldering with Bobbi Bensman / Bobbi Bensman. — 1st ed.
       p.   cm.   (Climbing specialists)
    ISBN 0-8117-2677-0
    1. Rock climbing.   2. Bensman, Bobbi.   I. Title.   II. Series.
GV200.2.B47   1999
796.52'23—DC21
                                                                97-25955
                                                                CIP

Contents

1. My Story 1

2. Moving on the Rock 9

3. More Moves 22

4. Preparing to Climb 35

5. Competing 59

6. Climbing Safely 64

7. Ethics 74

Glossary 81

Acknowledgments

A special thanks to my mother and father for all their love and support. And to my brother, Todd, a professional journalist—thanks for the encouragement to write this book.

And to Dale Bard, Mari Gingery, and Jimmy Surette for showing me the light.

And to Lynn Hill for the first female ascent of Midnight Lightning, a famous boulder problem in Camp Four, Yosemite National Park. It sat there unclimbed by a woman for twenty-one years!

And to all of my numerous bouldering partners who caught me in mid-air so many times.

And to the gods and goddesses above, please, please reopen Hueco Tanks State Park, El Paso, Texas!

An Important Note to Readers

This book contains much useful information about the sport of bouldering. Before engaging in this potentially hazardous sport, however, you must do more than read a book.

This sport requires skill, concentration, physical strength and endurance, proper equipment, knowledge of fundamental principles and techniques, and unwavering commitment to your safety and that of your companions.

The publisher and author obviously cannot be responsible for your safety. Because bouldering entails the risk of serious and even fatal injury, we emphasize that you should not begin climbing except under expert supervision. No book can substitute for proper training and experience under the guidance of a qualified teacher.

– 1 –

My Story

I was born and raised in the cosmopolitan yet very Texan city of Houston—where there wasn't a mountain in sight! My younger brother, Todd, and I grew up in a traditional middle-class family and had what you would call a normal upbringing. My father sold insurance and mutual funds while my mother stayed home until we kids were in high school; she then began a successful career in real estate.

Both my parents came from academic upbringings, so I knew as a kindergartner that I would go to some major university somewhere, someday. My parents really encouraged Todd and me in school, but only Todd was pushed into the world of athletics. He was nudged to play Little League baseball and football; I was urged to try cheerleading, which gave me my first taste of real competition. I'll never forget how stressful it was to work so hard on a cheerleading routine, perform it in front of a board, and go against a hundred other girls for only five places on the squad. I guess this was also my first experience with focused training, an experience that has served me well in my climbing career. I made the squad and will always remember the feeling of success and the rush of confidence I got. Now, of course, I think, "all that just to cheer for the boys?" How lame.

I did well in junior high school, but had a bout with drug addiction and was put into a drug rehabilitation program called Palmers Drug Abuse Program, where I struggled to regain my sobriety in a setting with other kids my age. It was a twelve-step program that really helped those who wanted to end their relationship with drugs. My successful battle against addiction is one of the biggest victories of my life.

While I was still in junior high school my parents decided to move from Texas to Phoenix to be closer to the rest of the family. (My mother's father was the head casino manager for the MGM Grand in Las Vegas, a five-hour drive from Phoenix.) I don't think my parents realized how hard a move like this can be for an adolescent. It sure was tough on me. I arrived at my new school in the middle of the semester and found the other students to be cliquish and not too interested in welcoming me. I don't believe I was ever comfortable there.

In my senior year, to try and fit in, I decided to run for student body secretary. I was determined to win and threw myself into campaigning. I put up posters and flyers all over school—only to see them defaced with swastikas. (My family is Jewish.) That was not the first time I had dealt with anti-Semitism, nor would it be the last. I lost the race to the former secretary, but I think I learned more about life after losing the election than I would have if I'd won. My racial awareness was aroused, and I started to take a long, hard look at all types of discrimination all over the globe. I've never forgotten those swastikas.

That same year I hooked up with some neighborhood friends who were keen on this act they called rock climbing. I begged them to take me along on one of their outings; they finally did—and my whole life changed. We went to an area north of Phoenix known as the Carefree Boulder Pile (today it's a golf course with no climbing allowed—heinous!). The first route I did was a bolted (quarter-inch bolts) 5.4 called Renunciation. No sticky Sportivas then: I wore big, crazy hiking boots and a harness made of webbing. I was on top rope. I loved it.

Maybe it was a form of rebellion to shock my parents and punish them for not encouraging me to be an athlete. (Who knows, if I had won that election, I might be a politician today—the cash flow would probably be better.) Maybe it was because I suddenly felt free to be my own person, something I've always tried to do. Whatever it was, from that day on all I wanted to do was eat, sleep, and breathe climbing. I climbed each and every weekend the remainder of my senior year and over the holidays I went up to Granite Mountain in Prescott and Joshua Tree National Monument. I began leading my second weekend out, and to this day I still love every aspect of climbing.

My parents, of course, were quite concerned—distressed, actually. Years later my brother told *Rock & Ice* that at the time my folks were "hoping and praying" that I would put an end to this climbing nonsense and move on with my life. They really wondered what had happened to their daughter and where exactly their upbringing had gone so wrong. My climbing partners all looked like hippies, which certainly didn't help matters.

Todd was supportive, though. He told the *Rock & Ice* writer that he thought it was really cool that I had taken this detour and fallen head over heels in love with this alternative lifestyle. "She went wherever the sun was," he said.

There was lots of sun in Phoenix in the summer of 1980. I had graduated from high school and had been accepted by the University of Arizona in Tucson for the fall semester. I had money saved from working at Desert Mountain Sports and three whole months to play. I went to Yosemite, pitching my tent in the world-renowned Camp Four. It was in this amazing national park that I really began my climbing adventures. I did the Royal Arches, a multipitch 5.6, 1,300 feet high. I bouldered all over Camp Four. I loved everything about Yosemite—the amazing walls, the beautiful flora and fauna (pines and bears), and all the freaky people!

The other Yosemite climbers were impressed with what I as a novice was doing and they gave me no small dose of praise and encouragement. Their support really boosted my self-confidence; I had never really gotten such encouragement for my athletic accomplishments before. My newly formed muscles also boosted my confidence. I've seen climbing have this same effect on many other women and girls. The athletic effort, the successes, the toned body, and the camaraderie of the climbing community do wonders for their self-image.

In September, psyched from my three months in Yosemite, I entered college, excited by the new experience and inspired by the looming peaks of Mount Lemmon, which I could see from my ninth-floor dorm room. Soon after I registered for classes, I started exploring the mountain's beautiful spires, south-facing walls, and north-facing domes. Rising above the Tucson valley, Lemmon offers climbing at elevations from 2,900 to 9,000 feet. The scenic Mount Lemmon Highway goes through four wonderful ecosystems—you start surrounded by saguaro cacti and end up surrounded by tall pines—and makes getting to the best climbing spots easy. I didn't limit myself to the climbing up on Lemmon, however. There were some awesome "buildering" opportunities available on the U of A campus, which I took advantage of, to the great interest of the university police and local media.

I graduated in 1986 with a double major in Sociology and Women's Studies, and also, if the truth be told, from the University of Mount

Lemmon, with honors. After five years, my climbing skills had really improved. But the "real world" soon became a bit overwhelming. I had no idea what I wanted to do with the rest of my life, or even with the rest of the year.

I soon found at least a few answers. For my senior thesis, I had spent three days a week doing volunteer work at the Tucson Center for Women and Children, a shelter for battered women. The center offered me a full-time job as a counselor, and I soon found that an effective way to inspire some of the women I worked with was to introduce them to climbing up on Mount Lemmon.

I worked there for a year, then decided I needed a change, so I moved to the eastern side of the Sierra Nevada Mountains, to the small (5,000 people) town of Bishop, California. I got a job selling outdoor gear at Wheeler & Wilson's, now Wilson's Eastside Sports. Bishop opened up a whole new climbing life for me. The Buttermilks—one of the best bouldering areas in the country—was only six miles away. Yosemite was close by as well, and every weekend I would drive over Tioga Pass and climb in the spectacular Tuolumne Meadows and the "Valley." Oh, what heaven I was in! I could smell the sagebrush every day, soak in hot springs, climb on granite domes . . .

I soon met my "guru" in Bishop—Dale Bard, one of my all-time favorite heroes of climbing and an incredible boulderer (he's really a master of all kinds of climbing). We hooked up and started bouldering together—mostly at Deadman's Summit near Mammoth and closer to home, in the Buttermilks. My climbing skills took off. I learned a lot about the sport, my finger strength improved, and I gained all-around power. I was simply in love with bouldering. I found all kinds of great problems all through the Buttermilks. I could do challenging circuits that took just a half hour or four full hours. I played, explored, pro-jected, did whatever I wanted to do.

I was also into roped climbing. Back in 1980, on my first trip to Yosemite, I had longed to try ascents of Astroman, the Rostrum, the Nose Route on El Capitan, and the Northwest Face of Half Dome. I can still remember when I heard that Molly Higgins and Barb Eastman had made the first female ascent of the Nose Route on El Capitan—I was so taken with these two women's accomplishment, inspired beyond belief. (Years later, while bouldering at Rockreation in Salt Lake, I learned that Eastman was in the gym—under the same roof! I went up to her like a starstruck groupie, introduced myself, and thanked her for helping me

Working The 7pm TV Show, Rifle, Colorado.

get to where I am today. It was a special moment for me.) And so I returned to Yosemite Valley in 1982, determined to climb El Cap and Half Dome. I quickly found a partner after posting signs at Camp Four. Looking back on those climbs, I realize they weren't the epic adventures they might have been (we had to sit out a huge storm on the Nose Route, but that's par for the course). Both climbs went smoothly, and I was especially happy to have swung leads with a man the whole way up.

The first Phoenix Bouldering Contest was held in April 1983 at Camelback Mountain in Scottsdale, Arizona. It was all bouldering, with a few top ropes here and there. I entered and, although I must admit that I can't remember the actual competition very clearly, I won. It was the first time I felt I could really compare myself with other women climbers. And there weren't that many women in the sport back then; males dominated. In 1982 I probably could have counted the number of really great women climbers on both hands: Beth Bennett, climbing hard in Eldorado Canyon in Colorado; Barbara Devine in the Shawangunks; Mari Gingery in southern California; Sue Patenaude in New Hampshire; Louise Sheppard of Australia; and, of course, Lynn Hill. All of these women were climbing solid 5.11s, and a few were climbing 5.12s. As few as they were, these women and their accomplishments meant the world to me. I owe them a lot. They gave me drive and motivation. I had incredible fire in my veins for climbing, and knowing there were other women out there pushing the limits made the sport come alive for me.

Since that first win at Phoenix, I've worked hard at climbing for almost twenty years now, enjoying my successes and trying to learn from my failures. I've done more than a hundred ascents of 5.13s, won some twenty national competitions, including twelve Phoenix Bouldering Contests, and have been a semifinalist in five World Cup Competitions. I've bouldered a handful of V9s.

I've also tried to promote climbing any way I can, giving workshops and seminars all over the United States—on training, technique, sport psychology, and other topics. I'm especially proud of a multimedia slide show I developed entitled "Of Power and Grace: A Celebration of Women and Climbing" that tours the country. This show tries to balance the scales a bit—after sitting through show after show presented *by* men and *featuring* men, I wanted to fill a gap and highlight women's contributions to the sport. So I put together a show that doesn't have a single dude in it! I've discovered that the show inspires men as much as it inspires women—which is great.

Bouldering alone in Castle Valley, Utah.

Now this book. Some of you might ask "why a book on bouldering?" One of the wonderful things about climbing is that there exist many paths, many branches on the tree—ice climbing, mountaineering, big-wall climbing, sport climbing, crack climbing, and bouldering, which, I am proud to say, is as strong a branch as any other. Climbing with others is great, but you can go bouldering solo—no partner, no gear, just you and the rock, and a pair of boots. I love the purity of the sport. And if time is short, you can get a killer workout in a matter of minutes.

Bouldering has always been the key part of my climbing career. It's good training, fun, social, soulful, competitive. Bouldering has made me a better all-around climber. It requires strength, focus, technique, explosive movement, and dedication to get to the top—skills that all kinds of climbing require. Bouldering has helped my free climbing immensely. It has also helped me develop the power necessary to win, to tackle difficult on-sights and red-points. Bouldering means all this to me, and I really want to help others discover what bouldering can mean to them.

I now live with my two cats in Rifle, Colorado, in the middle of climbing country, and I've been lucky to be able to climb in some of the best bouldering spots in the world—Yosemite; the Buttermilks; Hueco Tanks; and the Fontainebleau, the famous and beautiful bouldering forest south of Paris. But no matter where I go, I always seem to notice that women are sorely underrepresented in the sport. Some might say it's because bouldering requires such strength, but it also requires super technique, and women are every bit as capable as men at mastering it. And anyway, if women are weaker than their male counterparts, what better way to build strength than by bouldering? As women become stronger, their self-esteem takes off. I want to help make that happen.

I wrote this book to encourage and inspire. Whether you are male or female, tall or short, big or small, dog or cat, when you repeatedly fail on a boulder problem, maybe for days, even months, and then one day you finally send it, the feeling is absolutely awesome. There's nothing like it in the world.

Let's get going . . .

– 2 –

Moving on the Rock

First thing: get warm. When you boulder, you push muscles, tendons, joints, and ligaments to the max. To keep them from straining or pulling or tearing, you must warm up before you climb and do it the right way. A warm-up gradually increases your heart rate and blood flow, heating up muscles and connective tissue, making everything work better and preparing your body for what it's about to do. Cold muscles are more likely to get cramped, strained, or sore. Or to fail when you need them most.

Some climbers start stretching right away, believing that stretching is a good way to get warm. They're wrong. Cold stretching can damage muscles and tendons. It's best to ease into a workout with a full-body warm-up—slow jogging,

Tools of the trade: climbing shoes and a chalk bag.

stationary cycling, or light aerobics—for at least five minutes. When you break a light sweat, you know you're warm and ready to go.

I usually warm up by climbing: simple traversing or doing simple problems with big holds that are easy for me. I always start out slowly, getting the large muscle groups—biceps, chest, back, and deltoids—warm first. After I feel these big muscles warming up, I do some easy climbing that makes use of smaller handholds and footholds. This gets my tendons, ligaments, and joints warmed up, too.

Holds and Grips

Crimping. This is the basic way boulderers grab the rock. To crimp, take a hold with your fingers close together and bent at the first knuckle. It's a simple but effective technique that will let you hang on to some of the worst holds on the planet—incut flakes, microthin edges, even near slopers. Sometimes you can even find a groove or a little nubbin on a sloper that you hold onto by crimping.

You'll hold on better if you can get as many of your fingers on the hold as possible. Wrap your thumb over your index finger for a firmer grip. This also distributes the weight more evenly and places less stress on the other finger joints. The pinky will want to come off the rock when you crimp; at least it always does for me. It's important to keep as many fingers as you can on that crimp.

The crimp is an essential grip, but it requires a lot of arm and hand strength to use it effectively. Crimping also stresses the tiny tendons in the

Crimping.

Boulderers rely on good crimping technique.

Pinch grip.   Open-handed grip.

hand, putting them at great risk of injury. Crimping properly reduces your chances of getting hurt.

Pinch Grip. The pinch grip is a favorite of mine; I use it all the time. It's used when the only way to grip a hold is to pinch or squeeze it with your fingers or hands. To pinch properly, place four fingers on one side of the hold and the thumb on the other side—then squeeze as hard as you can. Like crimping, pinching requires strength that takes time to develop. Pinching sounds simple, but it does require practice to master and use effectively. Once you can do it right, you'll use pinching all the time. Pinch-gripping is a good way to protect an injured tendon; it's easier on the tendons than crimping and pocket pulling are.

Open-handed Grip. The open-handed grip is less stressful than the pinch grip, since it spreads the weight over more of the skeletal system of the hand. Open-handed grips can be completely open—with the fingers held straight, the fingertips not gripping anything at all—to near pinch grips. Open grips work great when the holds are giant, rounded, and slopey. Using a completely open grip is known as palming; the hand is flat and the entire palm is placed directly on the rock. Palming works because of the friction between the rock and the skin of the palm.

Leg lifts strengthen the torso.
A strong torso is key to
good bouldering.

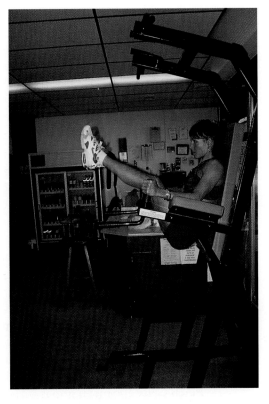

Moving the hand even a little breaks the friction, and the hand starts to slide—so don't move it.

A side note: When you're concentrating on your grip, don't become so focused that you forget to keep your torso strong and tucked in. The grip will be more effective if you keep up your energy from the sternum to just below the hips. When I climb, I think of that part of my body as a steel cable and try to keep it tight, especially when I take open-handed grips and pinches. Even with your feet on big, comfortable jugs, you need body tension to hold you in. The more powerful your abdominal area is, the easier it will be to keep yourself on the rock. (Ways to build strength in the abdominal area are covered in Chapter 4.) Good grips and tension in the torso will bring you much bouldering success. I promise.

Static Motion and Dynamic Motion

There are two basic ways the boulderer can move over vertical space: static motion and dynamic motion. Beginning boulderers tend to move statically almost all the time. The body freezes, a hand or foot moves to another hold, the body moves, locks off, then the hand or foot reaches again, and so on. Beginners usually concentrate on maintaining three points of contact with the rock while moving the fourth point, which is very deliberate and controlled and feels relatively safe. Experienced boulderers, too, fall back on using three-point contact climbing—especially when they are gripped out of their gourds—because it enables them to down-climb from a perilous position to safety, which is almost impossible to do using dynamic moves.

After beginners start to feel comfortable, they'll appreciate how dramatically dynamic movement can extend their range. "Dynos" are a way to reach holds that seem to be just beyond the climber's grasp. To do a dyno, the climber sinks slightly, then pushes off with the legs and whichever hand has the current hold, before reaching for the new hold with the other hand. The dyno's energy comes from the strength of the leg muscles.

You simply have to master dynamic movement to be a good boulderer (I admit it: dynos are one of my longtime weaknesses). Dynos are the only way to reach handholds that are far apart—beyond the reach of the climber who's trying to maintain three points of contact. They also can get you out of sticky situations: Let's say you just can't hold a locked-off position and at the same time reach up and feel for the next hold. And to make things worse, your present hold is shaky and you're starting to lose it. You spot a killer jug a few feet above you. It's definitely farther than you can reach, so you use momentum, jump up, and snag it! That's a dyno—an all-or-nothing move, a belief move. If you miss it, you hit the crash pad (but hey, life goes on).

Women sometimes shy away from doing dynamic moves. I've heard many say they're afraid because they feel they are too short. But it's shorter climbers—men and women—who can benefit the most from dynamic movement. It definitely should be a part of every climber's repertoire.

Dynos are also the key to making a big move from a solid hold. Say you have one supersolid hold and the next one is four feet above you and there's nothing but smooth rock in between. The only way to reach the hold is to do a gigantic jump: You need to make a dyno. A big part of doing dynos properly is sensing the best time to throw your hand up and snag the hold. You'll get the most height gain if you grab the hold at the absolute peak of the jump, the instant before you change direction, which is known as the "dead point." Just before gravity starts to pull you back down, latch the hold. It takes lots of practice to be able to sense the dead point. Believe in yourself; you can do it.

There are different types of dynos. The one described above is a single-handed dyno. A double dyno is when you lunge upward and reach with both hands—all four of your limbs come off the wall at once. A well-done double dyno is an unbelievable move. You are airborne,

Jimmy Surette executes a double dyno, one of the most exciting moves in bouldering.

moving upward, and at the very top of the flight, just before you start to drop down to the earth, you snag the hold with both hands.

The key to a good dyno is to get your feet in the proper position before you start your lunge. You want a firm, predictable push from the rock, so you need a solid base. It's important to experiment with foot placement. Sometimes you'll want your feet placed on lower holds, sometimes on higher ones. Don't fall prey to tunnel vision and look for the same type of foothold every time you set up for a dyno. Be creative and try everything. Every dynamic situation is different, and your footholds will need to be, too.

Indoor climbing gyms are great places to practice dynos. You can make up your own lunges and try them again and again until they're perfect. Start slow and build up your confidence and skills with smaller moves until you feel ready to try bigger lunges. I kid you not, once you get hooked on bouldering, you'll find that many of the world's greatest problems require lunges.

A dyno is a dramatic move that will improve your climbing skills enormously once you master it. But doing a dyno isn't always the best choice. You must carefully assess the risks involved to help you decide

Indoor training, a great way to practice dynos.

whether to dyno or not. If the only consequence of failure is a short drop on to a crash pad, you'll probably conclude that you have nothing to lose and go for it. On the other hand, if you are bouldering high above sharp, hard rocks, you might decide that the best choice is to *not* dyno and statically down-climb your way to safety.

The dead point (not the same dead point mentioned before) is a mini-dyno. In a true dyno, one or both feet come off the wall or rock. Usually in a dead point, the holds you are moving off of are poor and the hold you are moving to is just within reach, but you have to *thrutch* a bit in a dynamic manner to get there. When you dead point, your feet stay on the rock, but you're really using a dynamic motion to get to the next hold.

Good boulderers can dyno to and from a variety of grips—pinch grips, crimps, open-handed grips—and from laybacks and under-clings (described later in this chapter). Versatility is an important part of the sport.

Cross-Through Move

The cross-through move is the basic way boulderers move *across* the rock. Boulderers traverse—move vertically across the face of the rock—a lot more than conventional rock climbers do. In fact, sideways movement dominates some boulder problems. To cross-through, you grab a handhold with the hand farthest away from the hold—if you're moving to the right, you reach with your left hand, which puts your body in the correct position for the next move; it's really a set-up for the next sequence.

To imagine a climber moving across the rock using cross-through moves, picture six handholds between points A and B, going from left to right. One way the climber could tackle the sequence is to start with both hands matched on the first hold, move the right hand to hold #2, then the left to hold #2, then move the right hand to hold #3, then the left to hold #3, and so on all the way to hold #6. This adds up to ten hand movements—not the most efficient path.

But if the climber starts with both hands matched on hold #1, moves the right hand to #2, then crosses the left hand over to #3, the right hand over to #4, crosses the left hand over to hold #5, and ends with the right hand on #6, she's completed the sequence in only five hand movements. This efficient movement makes a big difference: five hand movements are way less fatiguing than ten.

Crossing through is a "hip" thing—each time you cross through you must keep your hip as close to the wall as possible. For example, reach far with your left arm across your body, keeping your left hip close to the wall, left foot in a backstep position. As soon as you gain the left hold, pivot your body to the exact opposite position. You don't want to "barn door" away from the wall, so once the hold is

Shelley Presson executes a cross-through.

gained, be ready to find a hold for the back-stepping right foot and
then roll the shoulders through. Voila! To me, a well-done cross-
through move feels very much like telemark skiing: pretty and pre-
cise, with no wasted energy.

One-Arm Lock-off

The one-arm lock-off stabilizes one handhold while freeing the other
hand to make a static movement. Say you have a hold with each hand.
With the hand you want to lock off, pull down hard and far. Keep your
body as close to the rock as possible, so your locked-off hand is close to
and at the same height as your shoulder. You're now in a better position
to move than if you were half bent. Also, keeping the locked-off hand
close to the shoulder takes advantage of your upper back muscles,
which are stronger than your arm muscles.

Sometimes doing a lock-off and moving statically is more energy-
efficient than throwing a dyno. Climbers who shy away from dynos are
usually lock-off masters, and vice versa, but it's best to be great at both,
so work to master the technique that's weaker.

Second Generation or "Bumping"

You have a solid right handhold and a good potential handhold (#1) in
the distance. You decide it's best to reach for #1 with your left hand so
you'll be in the proper position for the next sequence. Then you notice
an intermediate handhold (#2) a teeny bit lower than the first one you
saw. You see that #2 can help you gain #1, so in one smooth, quick, continuous motion you snag #2 with your left hand and then use your
momentum to gain #1 with the same hand. That's the quick double-
hand move called bumping, which seems like a real '90s fad, but is
actually something boulderers have done for a long time.

Gaston

The Gaston is a move that helps you make use of even the tiniest holds
the rock might offer, especially vertical handholds, or flakes. To picture
how you do a Gaston, imagine you have a five-inch-long vertical handhold. To make use of it you must place all of your fingers on it and push
it away from your body in the direction of the next hold. Sometimes, if
the hold is tiny, you can only get bits of your fingers on it. I use the Gaston a lot, even though it's a strenuous move that really puts my arm
and shoulder muscles to work.

One-arm lock-off.

Laybacking.

(Why's it called a Gaston? It's named after Frenchman Gaston Rebuffat, a climber, author, and film maker who was a pioneer of many modern climbing techniques.)

Laybacking

All boulderers depend on laybacking, especially when they're faced with sloping or vertical holds. It's tiring but energy efficient—a fundamental move all good boulderers have to master. I think of laybacking as kind of like climbing a palm tree, if you can imagine that. To layback properly, grab the lip of a crack, then bring your feet up and push straight into the rock. Pull with your arms and push with your feet to create opposing pressure against opposite sides of a crack. You need to find a comfortable middle position for your feet: too high and your arms won't be able to hold, too low and your feet will slip out. Move one limb at a time. Don't try big moves during a layback. Shuffle.

Underclinging

Underclinging is how you take an upside-down hold, one that faces the earth. Grab it with your palms facing skyward, fingers on one side, thumb on the other. You can undercling an edge, crimp, or sloper, but to do it effectively you'll need strong arm muscles. You'll know instantly if a climber does a lot of underclinging: they'll have bulging biceps.

Like in laybacking, the feet play an important role in underclinging. You want good footholds that offer a firm foundation. When you undercling, the less there is to stand on, the higher your feet need to be—this enables you to get more weight on your feet. To practice moving sideways on an undercling, shuffle one hand and one foot at a time.

— 3 —

More Moves

Manteling

Boulderers seem to forget that the fundamental move of manteling can often come in handy, especially when they find themselves on a severely sloping ramp or shelf—no edge, no grip, no nothing in sight—just below the top of a problem. You're up high, you've come far, you've got one more move to make; how do you finish?

You gotta mantel. Place both hands flat on the rock, wrists out, fingers pointing in. Pull yourself up so your chest is even with the top of the boulder, then lock off with one arm and place the heel of the other hand on the ledge, fingertips pointing inward toward the other hand. Cock the elbow of the arm not locked off up into a vertical position, as though you were going to support your weight with that arm. Do the same with the other arm—both elbows are now pointing to the sky. Push down until both arms are straight, then bring one foot up to support your weight. Press up to a standing position—staying balanced—and you've done it.

You can mantel nice edges, too, and you don't have to mantel with both arms. If one hand is on a solid crimp and the other is on a nice edge that's a little too low to help you reach the next hold, turn your fingers inward and mantel the hold.

Figure-Four Reach

The figure-four reach is not real common, but it can be effective in certain situations. It's a wild, long static move that can get you up as high as a dyno can. Say you have both hands on a jug and you want to get your left hand on a hold that's fairly far away. Lift the left foot and thread it between your hands, putting the foot then the leg over your right wrist; turn and twist until your crotch is resting on your right wrist. Now pull yourself into an upright position—the handhold that seemed so distant is now reachable.

The figure-four requires you to pull hard, so you definitely need to start with as friendly a hold as you can find. Even so, sharp edges cutting into your skin is a price you might have to pay to make the move. If you do it, beware of any sudden wrist pain; the figure-four puts tons of stress there.

Footwork

Footwork is often overlooked, but it's absolutely critical in bouldering. Some people think bouldering is strictly an upper-body sport. They're wrong. Masterful footwork and smart body positioning can make up for a lack of upper-body strength and allow climbers to do some amazing things on the rock. You don't have to be a superstar or a honed mama to be a great boulderer. Of course, it does help to have it all. But—for crying out loud—who *does* have it all?

Good footwork takes time to develop. Too often boulderers just slap their feet on the rock and then shuffle around looking for a solid hold. When they do this, they usually find the worst one. To learn good footwork, boulderers have to improve what I call their "eye-to-foot coordination." Here's how: Make sure you always place your feet on the best part of every foothold. Watch yourself do it. Take your time. Consciously look for and use the best part of each and every foothold. On real and artificial holds, look for tiny pits or slopes.

It's important to think "feet first." Establishing solid foot placements *before* making a move helps take pressure off the upper body. Flow up the rock like a stream of water, moving along the path of least resistance. Take advantage of everything you can. Let your lower body carry the weight whenever possible; leg muscles, especially the quads, are always stronger than biceps or pecs, no matter how many push-ups you do.

Smearing. Smearing is the footwork technique beginners are most familiar with. To smear, you put as much footsole rubber on the rock as possible to create friction that allows you to grip. Smooth slopes without edges require you to smear like crazy. To do it properly, place your foot on the part of the rock that slopes the least. Spread your weight solidly and evenly over the entire sole of your foot. If you push hard enough and keep your torso tense, you can get a good hold even on overhangs and vertical rock.

Smearing.   Edging.

Smearing is a belief move—you have to trust your technique. Sometimes your feet will sketch right off the rock and you'll be outta there. Experiment to build confidence. Also, try different kinds of boots with sticky rubber. Boots with soft or no mid-soles work best—*slip* last boots instead of *board* last boots.

Edging. Another basic foot technique is edging—butting the edge of your boot onto a mini rock ledge. Although you'll usually edge with the inside part of your foot, an inch or two from the toe, you can use all of the edges of your sticky rubber sole or rand. Carefully place the inside edge of your boot on even the smallest of features—you'll be surprised at how easily you can stand on them.

You'll use smearing and edging on steep rock, but you'll also need to use some fancier footwork.

Backstepping. Backstepping, long popular in France, is an effective way to extend your vertical reach. It involves butting the outside edge of your boot into nubbins or vertical edges while keeping your hip as close to the wall as possible. If you're reaching up with your hip against the wall, you'll get a lot more extension than if you face the wall straight on. Try it, you'll see.

So often climbers focus on using only the inside edges of their boots, which always puts their body in a straight-on position. Back-stepping adds variety to the climber's repertoire, but, to be honest, it's not always efficient, especially if the next handhold is far away.

In a straight-arm position, the climber will have to do one heck of a lock-off to gain that hold, which uses up a lot of energy. Try backstepping and using straight arms and rolling your hips to gain that hold instead.

Drop-Knee. A more intense version of the backstep—to do a drop-knee, put your foot on a vertical edge and then pivot, moving the inside part of your knee away from the rock, far enough so that your hip is against the wall and your knee is facing earthward. The drop-knee is especially useful on overhanging rock to hold your body into the wall and give you height.

Foot Dynos. When you're struggling with one strong foothold and two precarious handholds, maybe a pinch grip and a two-finger thin pocket undercling, your next best move might be to throw a foot up into the next hold: a foot dyno.

Step-Throughs. Crossing through with your feet (a step-through) just like you cross through with your hands is a great technique for traverses. I know it's tempting to match on every hold of a traverse, but step-throughs allow you to eliminate moves and save your energy. Efficiency is the name of the game. (You'll also look good doing it.)

Heel-Hooking. Heel-hooking—using your foot as a kind of third hand or claw—is another great technique for traverses. To heel-hook, raise your foot over your head and hook the heel of your boot over or behind any feature that looks like it will hold your weight. (Your hamstrings have to be well stretched to try this move.) Heel-hooking takes weight off your upper body, letting you cop a quick rest on the rock.

Remember that if you heel-hook in slippers, they tend to pull off; boots offer more support. Remember, too, that heel-hooking can be dangerous to your health. Don't forget to turn your heel-hook into a "toe-on" foot placement as you stand up to avoid damaging your inner knee, and to gain more height.

A similar technique, toe-hooking, is especially useful on overhanging rock. To toe-hook, use the toe of your boot the same way you would use your fingers in an upward pull. If you can hold this position and find something to push against, you are "push-pulling" or bicycling— one foot is pulling toward your body while the other pushes away. This

Shelley Presson doing a double drop-knee.

Heel-hooking.

technique, too, takes weight off your upper body, saving energy you may need later.

High Stepping. High stepping offers a good way to get some quick vertical height gain. Step up high and plant the inside edge of your boot or your toe, then put all your weight on that foot. Flagging the opposite foot out as you make a high step can help you stay balanced.

Warning: this move can be hazardous to your health! Many climbers, including me, have torn the medial meniscus, the soft cartilage surrounding the knee joint, while high stepping. Pain is the unmistakable warning sign that proceeding is a bad idea. If you feel even a slight twinge while high stepping, retreat and use another technique, a backstep or a drop-knee.

Knee-Barring. A knee bar is a jam that works well if the spacing of the rock is just right. To knee-bar, put your toe or foot on one hold and your knee up against an opposing corner, roof, or bulge. Flexing the calf muscle or pushing against the knee takes weight off your upper body; if the knee

bar is good enough, it can provide a no-hands rest. Even if the knee bar is a little shaky, it can still be useful for taking some weight off (a knee scum), which can let you make a quick shake out or a move forward.

Remember, knee bars can be extremely painful, especially if the rock is sharp. Wear long pants or kneepads to help protect your legs. Pull the pad up above the kneecap and use it as a thigh pad. I sometimes sew sticky La Sportiva rubber on my kneepad, which not only adds cushioning, but also makes me feel as if I stick

Knee bar using a padded right knee on The Egg V8, Hueco Tanks.

better in the jam. I've seen Chris Knuth climb while wearing cut-off Levis for this effect. Whatever works.

Flagging. Your body will tend to want to flag a leg out as a natural way to stay balanced during a move. Say you are rocking onto one foot in a high step. Flagging the opposite leg out behind creates proper balance by forcing your center of gravity downward. Flagging your leg inside does likewise.

There are quite a few footwork techniques and body positions that will help you tackle just about any bouldering problem you'll face. Learn and master them all and you'll have a full bag of tricks to take to the rock.

Crack Technique

Boulderers often encounter all kinds of cracks they can grip with the hands or the feet. They must know how to climb them. *Free Climbing with John Bachar,* another book in this series, offers a detailed look at crack-climbing techniques, including finger locks, finger stacking, and all types of jams.

Completing Boulder Problems

Onsight flashing is, to me, the purest form of climbing. The *onsight flash* is when you approach a boulder problem knowing absolutely nothing about how to solve it except what you can learn from studying the holds you can see, then, with no other knowledge of the hand- or foothold sequences, you do the route, start to finish, without falling. To me, the onsight flash is the ultimate—a beautiful thing, pure and free, just you and the rock.

In most cases, boulder problems are short enough and close enough to the ground that you can see every hold, especially if you follow the trail of chalk left by other climbers. While you're standing on the ground, you might be able to picture yourself moving from hold to hold, positioning your feet and body to solve the sequence in its entirety. If you can do this, you'll know exactly what you want to do before you jump on the boulder. As you climb, take note if what you planned to do really worked, or how you had to change the plan once you were on the rock. Learn from your mistakes.

If you do a boulder problem knowing the right moves in advance—if another climber has told you that the fourth move is a dyno with the left hand, for example, or if you've watched another climber send the problem—then that would be a *flash.* Not an onsight, but definitely a good effort.

Flagging outside.

Red-pointing a route is when you link all the moves from start to fin-ish without falling. You might have already tried to onsight the prob-lem, or maybe even flash it, and failed. So you went back to the drawing board, rehearsed all the necessary moves, and got to know the rock. Then you solved it—a red point.

I love red-pointing because it gives me an ongoing project to work on. I can wake up in the morning and have a mission, a problem I can focus on, confident that I'll succeed. That's the versatility of bouldering: it offers an in-the-moment workout or a work in progress.

Sometimes it takes a couple of tries to send a boulder problem; it might take years, or you might never get it right. I've flashed, onsighted, and red-pointed boulder problems all over the world, but there are plenty of problems still waiting for me to solve—in the Fontainebleau, Hueco Tanks, the Buttermilks. Some days you can't climb a thing, and you might have to wait weeks, months, or even years until you return to a particularly nagging problem. *Stick with it.* Believe me, it'll be worth the wait.

More and more climbers are into *beta-flashing,* which I must admit kind of bugs me. Beta-flashing is when a climber completes a problem by fol-lowing the instructions of peo-ple on the ground who tell you the moves: right hand to sloper, left to dime edge, and so on. The problem with this for me is that not all climbers are alike. What works for one climber might not work for another. There's usually more than one way to send a prob-lem. You have to do what works best for you.

Even I do some beta-flashing (Liz Grenard gives the beta).

Falling and Spotting

Bouldering by yourself can be a blast, but it's safer, more productive, and usually more fun to go with other people, especially if you're just starting out. Bouldering with others offers a more relaxed atmosphere in which you'll probably feel more comfortable pushing yourself and testing your limits. I think climbers should use as many spotters as it takes to ensure safety. Those who don't want to use a spotter because they think it shows weakness might be hurting their chances of success; they might not push themselves as hard as they would if they had a spotter. Spotters allow you to relax, concentrate on the climb, and push yourself harder without worrying about falling and getting hurt.

How to Fall. Falling is a part of bouldering, so falling properly is something every boulderer needs to know. Even if you have a dozen spotters, you must take responsibility for your own safety. You must always know how high off the ground you are and exactly where the safe landings are. When you are on lead or top rope, you can fall without much consequence,

but when you're bouldering, you must be able to jump off the rock and know how to land correctly. Try to land on both feet, keeping your balance. Bend your knees and sag into the landing so your knees aren't jolted on impact. Stay in control. Don't flail your arms; you might smack your spotter in the face.

Falling properly demands that you know where your body parts are in space, which takes practice. Learn to fall slowly, just as you would any other climbing skill. Do a single move and take a fall close to the ground. Add another move, and another, and before

Spotting a high problem.

you know it you're up high enough that a poor landing could do some damage. After your next move, you're up even higher, which can be intimidating. Learning to fall under control will give you the confidence to go on.

How to Spot. The spotter should always have both arms up and both feet solidly on the ground. He should always be moving to where he thinks the climber will land if he comes off the rock. Spotters don't necessarily have to camp out directly below the climber; if the climber is leaning left while doing a hard move, the spotter must move left of the climber's body while keeping an eye on his head. When the climber is close to the ground, the spotter should keep his hands close to the climber's head, preventing it from hitting the rock or the ground if a fall occurs. The spotter should shift his focus to the climber's waist as the climber goes higher; if the climber falls, the waist is where the spotter should try to catch—it's the climber's center of gravity. Even if the spotter misses, he should be able to cushion the fall and help the climber land on his feet.

If you can't catch a falling climber by the waist, try latching under the armpits. This can be a bit disgusting if the climber is wearing a tank top, but a brief, unpleasant experience is a small price to pay for saving a life or preventing an injury.

The number-one rule of spotting: Spotters must absolutely stay one hundred percent focused, even if some hottie walks by. Remember: a good spotter focuses exclusively on the climber—catching them if they fall, but otherwise not touching them.

Boulder Problem Ratings and Grades

Just like other kinds of climbing, bouldering has its own ratings system that grades the difficulty of various problems. In fact, it has several: the older French system uses B1, B2, and B3 grades; the "V" system, invented by John "Vermin" Sherman and used most commonly in the United States, goes from V0 (the easiest) to V13 (the most difficult).

The specifics of what makes a particular route a V8 instead of a V9 are tough to explain, and to tell you the truth, don't interest me much. I kind of wish we didn't have grades. In 1982, I did an ascent of the Left El Murray, on the north face of the Mushroom Boulder in Hueco Tanks. It was hard—it still *is* hard—and I was proud of my accomplishment. Years later I learned that the route has a rating of V6, which now makes it seem as though the climb is nothing particularly special. But when I did it all those years ago, it certainly seemed special to me.

Of course, we need grades so we can compare our climbs to other people's, see how much we improve, and know where to begin when we climb in a new area or gym. But I think it's important to keep from getting too caught up in grades and ratings. Remember that they are always subjective, and some are way off the mark. Remember too that if you're short, what's rated a V4 might really be a V8 for your size and reach. Take the ratings with a grain of salt.

I must mention that the Fontainebleau near Paris has a great way of showing the ratings of its numerous problems. They're all color coded, and you can follow circuit after circuit of the same color all through the forest. (Try the white; it's my favorite.)

– 4 –

Preparing to Climb

Diet

I try to eat a healthful, low-fat diet, but I'm not scientific or fanatical about it. I think that if you work out regularly you can eat almost anything you want. I love Thai and Indian food, and I don't stop myself from filling up when I go to a Thai or Indian restaurant. I don't think there's a problem with doing this every so often. My discipline kicks in when I'm training for a specific event or bouldering problem. I like to be a little lighter when I need to be, and I'll work to drop a few pounds if I think I should. (I always seem to drop a few pounds in the summer and gain a few back in the winter anyway; I think everyone does.) But I never count every calorie. I try to eat totally well—low on the fat and calories, lots of fruits and veggies, lots of fluid—about eighty percent of the time. I eat the not-so-good stuff twenty percent of the time—without going overboard. It works for me, and it keeps me from going crazy. But if you find that you do gain weight easily, you might have to keep a closer eye on the calorie count, or add more cardio workouts each week.

More protein and fewer carbohydrates—the so-called zone diet—seems to be the latest dietary trend, and I do follow it to a certain extent. I've found that I feel better when I increase the amount of protein in my diet. Because I eat only fish, no other meat, I make a lot of protein shakes with fruit, soy, or whey protein. I always take Clif Bars that have at least 9 grams of protein, fruit (pears, apples, bananas), and sometimes a can of tuna (which has 32 grams of protein) when I go out for a day of climbing.

Eat smart: I don't recommend that you go on any kind of extreme diet without consulting a doctor first. Make sure you know what you're doing and how your chosen diet will affect you before you start one.

I drink lots of water. (I personally don't trust tap water, so I'm always filling up my gallon containers at those 25-cent water stations. To me, distilled water tastes best.) Climbers need to drink plenty of water when they climb. Dehydration leads to slow muscle recovery, injuries, poor performance, and worse. I take along a giant Stanley thermos filled with hot herbal tea—no caffeine—if I'm out climbing in colder weather, when drinking plain water isn't too appealing. You need your fluids even if it's not hot.

Training

Before bouldering became a sport in its own right, traditional climbers, sport climbers, used to train by bouldering. The idea of doing specific exercises for climbing was almost unheard of until the '60s; before then, climbers simply climbed a lot of routes to train and keep in shape. I agree with this older philosophy to a certain extent: I think that the best overall training exercise for boulderers is to boulder. A lot. But in this day and age, to reach the very pinnacle of the sport, boulderers have to develop and stick with a sharply focused training regimen that includes exercise off the rock.

The ultimate goal of training should be to develop a full range of bouldering skills, not to develop bigger muscles (the bigger the muscles, the more weight you have to hoist up the rock). I've seen a lot of climbers make the mistake of working too hard on their muscles and not enough on their moves. A good training program should be balanced and geared to improve *all* the key attributes of a top climber: strength, power, suppleness, balance, endurance, technique, body tension, and last but definitely not least, mental fortitude.

Here's a typical week of training for me:

Monday

- Thirty- to forty-minute warm-up doing easy boulder problems.
- Two to three hours of hard bouldering, working on weaknesses.
- Short rest and a peanut butter Clif Bar (yum!).
- Drink a whole bunch of water.
- One-hour campus board session.

Tuesday

- Warm up by traversing on an easy wall, remembering to really stretch out my forearms and fingers.
- Twenty to thirty easier bouldering moves.

- Three hours of linking moves and red-pointing routes and boulder problems at or near my limit. Rest between laps until I am depumped and recovered.
- Stretch and cool down with easy courses.

Wednesday

- Get out of bed (this is harder than it sounds). This is a climbing rest day, but not a stay-in-bed day. One- to two-hour ride on the mountain bike or Stairmaster. The focus of this day for me is cardiovascular. You can substitute running or swimming with some other form of aerobic exercise.

Thursday

- Another climbing rest day. One-hour mountain bike ride or recumbent bike, just as long as the aerobic workout is a bit mellow compared to the day prior.
- Sauna and Jacuzzi if possible.
- Stretch and drink loads of water.

Friday

- Repeat Monday's routine of hard bouldering and campus board training.

Saturday

- Repeat Tuesday's routine of power-endurance bouldering.

Stretching

Whatever type of training program you adopt, it simply must include stretching. Personally, I like to combine two stretching programs—one for gymnasts and one for cross-country skiers—that I learned from Bob Anderson's excellent book *Stretching*. My flexibility program includes at least one exercise for each major muscle group. To increase flexibility, I stretch at least three times a week from ten to thirty minutes. To maintain the flexibility I gain, I continue the exercises at least once a week.

Here are some stretching tips:

- Jog in place for five minutes to warm up before you stretch. (Skipping the warm-up is probably the most common mistake.)
- Don't stretch immediately after a meal.
- Stretch on a mat or pad, not a slippery gym floor.
- Stretch one muscle group at a time.
- Move slowly and smoothly into each stretch.
- Keep your body properly aligned.

Stretching is a vital part of any climbing session.

- Relax and breathe. Exhale a bit harder when you move deeper into the stretch. Focus on feeling the stretch.
- Do each stretch two to six times; work up to ten or more.
- Don't bounce. Start by holding the stretch for five seconds. Then, as flexibility improves, hold the stretch longer, up to a maximum of sixty seconds. Don't hold the stretch until it hurts. Learn to distinguish between pain (bad) and high-level discomfort (okay). If a stretch is painful, stop.
- Come out of each stretch slowly and gently.

Forearm stretch.

Here are some basic stretches I recommend.

- With one hand, gently pull back the fingers on the other hand one by one. Hold for five seconds, then switch hands.
- Pull back all the fingers together to stretch the wrist. Do it palm up then palm down.
- Put your arms straight out to each side and make smaller and smaller circles in the air with your hands.
- Lace both hands together behind your back about waist high and bend at the waist. Lift your arms toward the sky.
- Hold your left elbow with your right hand and gently push your left biceps up to your chin. Hold for twenty seconds, then do the other side.
- Sit on the floor with the left leg straight out in front of you; put your right foot on the ground just to the left of your left knee. Twist your torso to the right. Hold for twenty seconds, then do the other side.
- Sit on the floor with your legs together, stretched out in front of you. Grab your toes and pull them toward you. Hold for five to ten seconds.
- Sit on the floor with your legs spread apart. Reach forward to touch the floor without bending your legs. Reach to one side, then to the other, holding each stretch for five to ten seconds.
- Touch your toes while standing. As you get more flexible, do it with your legs crossed. Hold for five seconds. Don't bounce! This is a good stretch for the hamstrings, but for some it can be hard on the lower back. If it is, lie on your back and slowly raise your leg up past vertical.

Weight Training

You can warm up and stretch without much guidance, but weight training is a bit more complicated, so it's best to get the advice of an expert to determine the specific weight-training program that's best for you. Some general tips to remember: Go slow at first and vary your exercises. If it's possible, use both resistance machines and free weights on alternate sessions. Work each body part hard once a week. Drink lots of water between sets. Use a weight belt when you do heavy lifting.

I try to stick to a weight-lifting program for at least eight weeks every year (usually over the winter, when I'm forced inside anyway), concen-

Pec-deck to work the chest.

trating on building power and strengthening muscles, especially the non-pulling, opposition muscles.

If I haven't lifted for ten months, I always begin *very* slowly, really concentrating on the muscle as it does its work. I like to rest at least three minutes between sets, but occasionally I need more time. Sometimes I can lift quickly.

When I lift, I focus on my breathing, exhaling during the lifting or contracting movement. It may not be ladylike, but I've found that if I grunt when I exhale during a big lift or difficult move it helps me concentrate my efforts.

The first week of weight training I use low weights and do more reps, with a max of three sets of exercises for each muscle group. It's a gradual start that eases both my mind and my body back into the lifting groove, helping me get ready for the weeks ahead, when I increase the weight and decrease the reps.

I always do at least twenty minutes on the Stairmaster or stationary bike to raise my heart rate and warm my muscles before I lift. Then I do at least ten minutes of deep stretching. When I have a good sweat going, I'm ready for the iron.

My first week of weight lifting might look like this:

Monday: Chest and triceps, 3 exercises/3 sets each, with a weight I can lift for 15 to 20 repetitions. Chest exercises: flat bench press; incline press; cable crossovers; pec-deck. Triceps exercises: cable pull-downs; kickbacks (with cable or dumbbells); dips; seated dumbbell triceps extensions.

Wednesday: Back and biceps, 3 exercises/3 sets each. Back exercises: lat pull-downs, both one and two arm (vary the spacing of the hands on the bar to work the muscles in different ways); bent-over dumbbell rows; seated long pull. Biceps exercises: machine biceps curls; cable or barbell curls; concentration curls; lying down cable curls.

Friday: Shoulders and legs, 3 exercises/3 sets each. Shoulder exercises: upright rows with bar or alternating dumbbells; standing side lateral raises with machines or dumbbells; standing front lateral raises; military press; shoulder shrug. Leg exercises: seated machine leg curls or leg extensions; horizontal leg or hamstring curls; leg press with machine.

A lot of climbers build their upper bodies and ignore working their lower bodies, thinking that heavy, muscle-bound legs will hamper their efforts on the rock. But high stepping, backstepping, Egyptians, and lots of other advanced techniques torque the hip and knee joints, so the muscles surrounding these joints have to be strong so the moves are effective and don't cause injury. Don't worry; if you do lots of leg repetitions—even fifteen to twenty—you will not grow big leg muscles!

For the second week of weight training, I add another set to each muscle group and begin doing fewer repetitions with more weight. By the third week, I'm doing one warm-up set and three heavy sets per exercise, with four exercises for each large body part (chest, legs, and back) and three for each small body part (triceps and biceps). To target

Side lateral raise to work the shoulders and delts.

Bent-over rows to work the lats and biceps.

the upper body, I do eight to ten repetitions; for the lower body, I do twelve to fifteen reps. The workout should be balanced; working only some muscle groups and ignoring others results in uneven muscle development and increases the chances for injury. Work both the muscles on each side of a joint. Some important opposing muscles: the biceps and triceps in the upper arm, quadriceps and hamstrings in the thigh, and pectorals and latissimus dorsi in the torso.

Exercising the Abdominals

Every athlete needs strong abs to stabilize and power the body for virtually every type of athletic activity. The abs are the key to transferring force between your upper and lower body. Strong abs are how climbers maintain the body tension they need to keep themselves on difficult holds. Strong abs also form a natural girdle that supports the lower back. You cannot have a healthy back or good posture or be a top-notch climber if you don't have strong abdominals. And boy does a strong stomach look sexy!

I work my abs continuously because I think it's one of my weak areas. I really focus on them during the winter, when I usually join a health club that has machines and incline boards that let me do a great ab workout. At home or during the fall, spring, and summer, I keep working, sometimes using an ab video on my VCR. (I've even copied ab workouts onto cassettes so I can listen to them on the road.)

I always do my ab work at the end of a workout, and I always start with the lower abs. Be patient: abs don't develop quickly. If you're consistent and persistent, you'll see results in four to six weeks. After that, when your feet cut loose on an overhang, you'll really notice the better abdominal control you've developed. And you'll look great in that bikini or those board shorts.

Following are some great ab exercises. Do three, four, or five sets of at least ten reps each. As you get stronger, you should try to do as many reps as you can.

Cobra Stretch. A good warm-up. Pelvis on the floor; support with hands next to hips. Arch your back, pulling the back of your head toward your heels. Cobras stretch the abdominal area and loosen up the lower back.

Reverse Curl. Lie on your back with your knees together and raised to the chest. Hold your arms straight up and bring your knees to your elbows, then push them away—that's one rep. Keep your shins parallel to the floor. Ankle weights or a decline board makes things more challenging.

Reverse curls to work the abs.

Cobra stretch.

Straight Arm Hang. Hang straight and motionless, facing the wall, from two solid handholds. Don't let your legs swing, if possible. (A partner might need to offer some support or help keep you still.) Twist to one side and raise both knees until your thighs are parallel to the floor. Then lower your legs. That's one rep. Now bang out nine more, then do the other side. Remember to move slowly and deliberately. As your strength increases, add ankle weights, increase your repetitions, or try awkward positions, like pointing your toes in different directions, or try to lift your legs even higher. Be alert for shoulder pain.

Crunches. The sit-up is dead; long live the crunch, the safest, most efficient way to condition abdominal muscles. Crunches condition the layer of muscle that covers your midsection, which often needs work; they don't work muscles that are usually strong to begin with, like the hip flexors. Unlike sit-ups, crunches are easy on the small of the back.

Technique is everything with crunches. Doing fewer properly is better than doing a lot improperly. Quality beats quantity on this one. To do the basic crunch, lie on your back, knees bent, feet flat on the floor. Lace your fingers together and put your hands on the back of your neck, just below your skull, to support your head. Point your elbows forward. Now focus on using your abdominal muscles to lift your upper body straight up, no higher than the bottom of your shoulder blades. Let your hands support the weight of your head. Hold the crunch for a count of three seconds, then release it. Repeat. Start with

two or three sets of ten reps, then gradually increase the length of time you hold the crunch and the number you do.

Modify the crunch to make it easier by holding your arms out in front of you. Make things tougher by pointing your elbows out or folding your arms across your chest.

No matter how you crunch, don't jerk your neck up.

Diagonal crunches work the obliques, the muscles that shape the sides of your abdomen or waist and provide the power for twists and turns. To do diagonal crunches, pull across your abdomen instead of straight up. Start with one foot

Hanging leg raises.

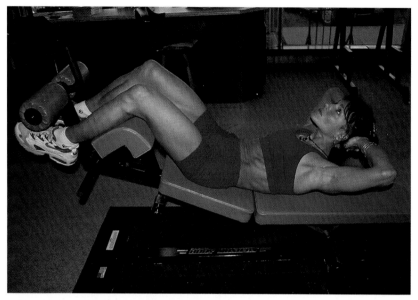

Killer crunches work those abs.

on the floor and the other resting on the opposite knee, hands behind the head and elbows out. Twist your right elbow toward the raised left knee. Do complete sets on one side before switching to the other.

Campus Boards

Campus boards range from three to twenty feet long and feature smooth wooden dowels placed horizontally on a wooden board, one on top of another, with varying distances between them. Using campus boards to train is a great way to increase strength, but it's also a great way to damage your tendons, even if you're a veteran climber. Don't campus until you have solid climbing experience under your belt—two years minimum; five years is better. Your muscles and tendons really have to be ready for a good yanking. A training expert at the gym is the best person to let you know when you're ready to campus. When you do campus, do it properly. Don't do it more than once a week to start (I never campus more than twice a week, and I try to rest for at least two full days between each session). Don't climb down rung by rung; doing so stresses the inner elbows. Instead, climb up and then jump down onto a mat. Be alert to any weird pains.

My campus board session might go like this: I warm up (always!), then do five or six ladder laps—ascents only and on the biggest rungs there are (usually there are four sizes, from micro-dowels to two-inchers). Between laps I rest for two or three minutes. Then I move to the next smallest rung and work on Plyometrics—one hand stays put while the other hand moves between an upper and lower rung—as well as lock-offs and double dynos. I try to do at least four to five sets of each on every rung. The smallest rung is the toughest, but I give it my best shot. I rest after each set as long as I need to. Sessions usually last an hour to an hour and a half, and that includes all of the resting as well.

Bouldering as Training

The more you boulder, the better boulderer you become. This seems pretty obvious. If you work difficult bouldering problems, the specific muscle fibers you use on the problems break down and rebuild, making them stronger. Performing difficult moves—especially short, explosive ones—then becomes easier. Experts call this the principle of specificity.

Getting out and bouldering two or three times a week is an ideal way to train. If the weather is nasty, do it indoors at the local climbing gym. Resist the impulse to do much more than that, however. The principle doesn't work if you don't give your muscles enough time to repair themselves; you won't be able to climb with all-out effort. On the other hand, if you boulder fewer than two times a week, you won't improve as much as you could.

Make bouldering a part of your training. Uniweep Canyon, Grand Junction, Colorado.

When you boulder to train, work specific muscles by changing the way you reach for holds. Lunge to do a static move. Lock off as high as you can to reach a hold you normally get to with a dyno, and so on.

One problem with training by climbing year-round in an indoor gym is that things can get boring and routine. Your training sessions will be more beneficial if you invent games to keep things interesting and challenging. I play "the bouldering game" (not a real original name, I know) with friends; we make up problems and challenge each other to solve them. We keep moving, but with three or four in a party, everyone gets enough rest. If the problems are good, I might tape them up to have circuits to do when in the gym.

Gather together a good group of climbers who are all at roughly the same skill level and set up a regular time to climb competitively. Take turns being the course-setter. (With moveable holds, this is an art in itself.) Award some kind of prize to the winner or the person who improves the most—dinner, gear, margaritas. Keep it fun—if it isn't fun, you won't stay with it.

To train outside, I sometimes go to a bouldering area and try to climb as many problems as I can in an hour or two. I try to include some very hard problems—too hard to complete in one or two tries. Within the time period, I make sure to rest and drink lots of water to stay sharp. At the end of the time period, I've done a lot of climbing and had a killer workout without using up half the day. Bouldering is the best for that.

I'll also make up bouldering circuits, linking five problems in a row, for example, back to back without resting. Then I try to do each circuit five times. I rest for three or four minutes between each set. If I succeed, I've done twenty-five bouldering problems in a short amount of time. Talk about a major pump! This is a good power-endurance workout as well. (If you do this, keep tabs on your heart rate so you don't keel over.)

The Cool-Down

Many climbers pack up and head for the car as soon as they're done climbing for the day. Bad idea. Cooling down after a bout of hard exercise is every bit as important as warming up. Easing your body back into a relaxed state keeps the blood from pooling in the muscles, helping them keep from getting stiff and sore later on. If you stop exercising suddenly, you're liable to get dizzy or faint. Fifteen minutes of easy traversing is a great way to cool down after a hard climb. Stretch during the cool-down; your muscles are warm, and it's a great time to increase your flexibility.

Sticking to a Schedule

These days, indoor gyms and woodies allow dedicated climbers to stick to an ambitious schedule all year round. They help you stay sharp all the time, but they also offer a temptation to overdo it. When I'm trying to get back into form after time off, I usually climb two days in a row, rest a day, then climb two more, and so on. After a few cycles of this I usually need two days off in a row. With hard bouldering or power training, I add more rest days to the mix.

I like to keep a journal of my climbing experiences, including training notes, which helps me develop a sensible schedule. Journaling gives me consistency, focus, and feedback on how I'm climbing and what I'm thinking. This information helps a lot if I'm coming back from an injury. Journaling is also a good way for me to monitor my progress on a particular boulder problem. It's all right there in black and white: whether I'm working too hard (if I notice that I've climbed five days this week, six the week before) or not hard enough (if I see that I'm spending more time in the hot tub than on the rock).

Cable cross-overs for the chest.

Rest

I've seen both beginners and experts throw themselves into a training regimen with reckless abandon, mistaking rest for laziness. What they're forgetting is that strength is developed during rest, not during exercise, as muscle tissue rebuilds. Hard exercise tears the body down; rest allows it to build back up stronger than it was before. Without days off or light days after hard days, your workouts are less productive and your climbing is less likely to improve. And if you don't rest, you're more likely to get injured. If you're constantly fighting any of the following symptoms, you might be working out too hard: a tendency to catch colds easily, chronic sniffles, headache, persistent soreness, lethargy, apathy, clumsiness, or a hung-over feeling from the previous workout.

A Special Regimen

At the end of 1994, my climbing skills seemed to plateau. I had a lot of quality climbs under my belt, but my red-points were stuck at 5.13b. I had unfinished 5.13c's all over the world! To get better, I decided I had to develop a new approach to my sport.

At the time, I was living in Salt Lake, where it seems that every climber is heavy into training. Doug Hunter, the head climbing instructor at Rockreation Climbing Facility, and I worked out a special five-month periodization program for me adapted from the regimen Dale Goddard and Udo Neumann spell out in their book, *Performance Rock Climbing*. The program had three parts—endurance, power, and power-endurance—and each part was divided into activities ranging from thirty minutes to two hours. Here's what I did.

The Vacation. The first thing I did was take a month-long break from climbing—a complete mental and physical vacation from my sport. I really think every climber should do this once a year. I did other activities to stay in shape; I spent time with my family. When you're really into climbing, you don't realize how all-consuming the sport can be. There's no off season. During a climbing break you can focus on other physical activities that will help you climb better—it's a great time to pump some iron. Just don't climb.

Phase One: Endurance. After my "vacation," I felt rejuvenated, ready to begin a seven-week endurance phase. It's important to start a training program with a focus on endurance because starting with power after a layoff can tweak your muscles and tendons. Ease back into things. (I found that my journal at this time was extremely helpful; it really let me know if I was doing too much too soon.)

For the four weeks of the endurance phase I did ten activities a week, plus jogging or another cardiovascular activity three or four times each week. Seven of the ten activities were aerobic restoration and capillarity (ARC) exercises, consisting of thirty to forty minutes of constant climbing—traversing, moving up and down the wall, and so on—at forty percent effort.

By varying my climbing routine during the ARC sessions, I was able to improve my technique as well as my endurance. For example, I climbed with only one hand as I traversed a wall or went up and down easy routes in the gym to improve my dynamic technique, or I used the lightest possible hand pressure, or only two or three fingers. Sometimes I would pretend I was an Indian and climb as quietly as possible.

The other three activities in the endurance phase were more intense: I tried to flash moderate boulder problems or routes (limited to three tries at most) or took turns with another climber on 5.10s and 5.11s.

I tried to rest at least two days each week during the endurance phase. In the final three weeks I added two bouldering workouts a week to prepare for my next phase, power.

At the time, I was totally focused on improving quickly, so I probably went at it too hard. If I were to do the same program now, I would definitely tone it down a bit, making sure I got more rest in between sessions. To be honest, I might seriously consider eliminating some or even all of the ARC sessions. Doing just volume is probably sufficient. Lots and lots of climbing, but at an easier level.

Phase Two: Power. I felt comfortable limiting the power phase of my training program to four weeks because power has always been my strong suit. I did at least twelve workouts a week with three rest days. I did three ARC sessions, two variable endurance, five bouldering, and two or three threshold sessions a week. Here, too, I might have overdone things a bit. It probably would have been smarter to cut out one or two activities. Doing too much doesn't let your muscles recover sufficiently. (Learn from your mistakes.)

Variable endurance consisted of thirty- to forty-minute sessions of continuous climbing. I climbed progressively harder problems and routes to a high point and then did easier problems back down. I completed two loops in about thirty minutes.

My bouldering sessions were usually sixty to ninety minutes of pretty hard bouldering—fun times with friends in the gym. The problems had three to eight moves; in between problems I would rest until I was depumped. I didn't strictly limit the number of moves—if I wanted to do more than eight on a particular day, I did.

Threshold bouldering, or maximum muscle recruitment, consisted of thirty, sixty, even ninety minutes of hard bouldering. Doing this, I was able to stay on the rock for only one to three moves at a time. I did a lot of air time, which wasn't much fun, but threshold climbing is the best training I know for muscle recruitment.

I worked with a partner during threshold bouldering, having them support part of my weight while I did moves that were above my capabilities; as I worked to master the moves, my partner gradually reduced the amount of weight they supported. This helped me increase the maximum load my muscles could hold.

Remember that the key to climbing is strength-to-weight ratio, so you don't have to have huge muscles to climb well. You just have to be well-toned and strong. And the only way to tone or strengthen a muscle is to overload it by placing a greater-than-normal demand on it. Three popular power training activities—pull-ups, weight lifting, and fingerboard workouts—do just that.

Climbing is also a pulling sport, a hand-strength sport, and the most effective way to increase your pulling strength is by doing standard two-arm pull-ups on a horizontal bar. Establish a baseline; see how many you can do. Then gradually do more. Increasing how often, how long, or how hard you exercise is the simple, basic way to increase your strength. (Note: Pull-ups strain the inner elbow; if you feel pain here, you're pushing too hard. Ease up.)

How often should you exercise? The accepted answer is that you should exercise a muscle three to four times each week to achieve significant gains in strength and tone without overworking it. Exercise carefully and conscientiously; don't wear yourself out. Adopting the strategy of many bodybuilders—working out five or six days a week, but exercising different muscle groups on successive days—will allow you to stick to a challenging regimen without stressing out your muscles. Devote three sessions a week to the upper body, two sessions a week to the lower body. Vary the pace of your workouts, pushing hard and fast some days and slowly and deliberately on others. Listen to your body.

On Dumpster BBQ, Rifle.

How long should you exercise? The length of your training session should vary according to what you want to accomplish. A starting workout of eight or ten basic exercises might take twenty to thirty minutes. A more advanced program might go forty-five minutes or longer and include exercises for specific problem areas.

How hard? Take it easy at first. If you haven't exercised for awhile, do a few reps of the easiest versions of each exercise. Gradually work up to ten reps without straining. Once you can do ten, rest a minute, and then start a second set. After you can do ten reps on the second set, rest and start on a third set. This third and last set should exhaust your muscles.

As your strength improves, doing three sets won't be enough to fatigue you. You'll have to add a fourth set or overload your muscles in one of the following ways:

- Make the exercises harder. Many basic exercises have variations that increase the load of your body weight on working muscles. If you're lifting weights, increase the amount.
- Don't rest so long between sets. With less time to rest, muscles must work harder to lift the same amount of weight.
- Do more reps in the last set. By doing more than ten, you will increase muscle endurance, which enables your muscles to make a sustained effort.

Phase Three: Power-Endurance. The final stage of my training regimen, the power-endurance phase, lasted seven weeks. I've always felt that power-endurance was my main climbing weakness. I was always too pumped to hang on for more during the red-point and the onsight.

The stage consisted of continuing the same power activities I had been doing and adding two more bouldering circuits. These were ultra-grueling but really paid off in the long run. Each circuit was five to eight continuous difficult boulder problems followed by a two-minute rest between sets. A single workout was five or six sets of a single circuit. Each set took thirty minutes, with about three minutes rest between sets. During this power-endurance phase I made sure to include two or three rest or easy climbing days per week.

I added "four by fours" to my training program in 1998. They've been incredibly helpful. Here's how I do them. I choose four boulder problems that are pretty steady for me. I do all four in a continuous row with two-minute rests between sets—that's four boulder problems in a

Training on the rock at Arapiles, Victoria, Australia.

row, two minutes of rest, four problems again, two minutes rest until I've done four sets total; hence, a four by four.

You can also do the same on routes. Choose four routes, making them so difficult that you are falling off toward the end of the workout. (Do this on top rope—it's too fatiguing for leading.) Do the first route four times in a row. Rest three to five minutes, then move on to the second route, and so on. These exercises aren't the same. The boulder problem exercise is short and intense, more on the power/resistance side; the route exercise is more power-endurance/endurance. Both are great, intense activities that keep you from getting bored in the gym. You'll be surprised at the holds you can actually recover on after you get a few of these exercises under your belt.

For the last days of my training, I reduced my bouldering sessions to two per week and my threshold bouldering to once a week. I increased my bouldering circuits to three per week.

After eighteen weeks of disciplined training, I was eager for the payoff, namely, peak performance rock climbing. I expected to do well. I hadn't skipped one activity; in fact, I threw in a few extras. At first, I was disappointed. I wasn't climbing well and thought that I might have overtrained. Then, after about six weeks of outdoor climbing three to four days a week, I recovered and started peaking. My climbing ability skyrocketed. By June I was really cranking and that summer I redpointed my first three 5.13c's!

The training program eventually paid off, but only after I toned it down a bit and included some catching up on rest and recovery. Just a reminder that you can have too much of a good thing.

Mental Training

I've learned a lot about an effective mental approach to bouldering from the book *Thinking Body, Dancing Mind* by T'ai Chi master Chungliang Al Huang, and Jerry Lynch, which I think should be required reading for any serious athlete. The book describes a Taoist approach to athletics, a combination of Western and Eastern philosophies specifically geared to athletes.

One of the most important parts of athletic success is the ability to focus, which isn't as easy as it sounds. When you're on the rock, random, distracting thoughts sometimes seem to fly at you from all directions. "My new boots are pinching." "Is my spotter paying attention?" "I wonder what I'm going to have for dinner." All of this wasted mental energy detracts from your full potential as a climber.

Liz Grenard demonstrates focus and concentration.

Focus, like dynos or backstepping, takes time and effort to master. It cannot be forced, but it can be learned so that it comes naturally when you climb. Two related ways to improve your focus are to associate positively and visualize success. Positive association involves dwelling on the positive so that you'll be distracted from the negative. Before a tough climb, think about past climbs when you were really cruising. Remember what it felt like, looked like, sounded like. Try to create as detailed a picture as you can, then immerse yourself in it.

Visualization involves mentally rehearsing moves before you do them. Link them together in your head, imagining the climb as one fluid experience. When you begin the climb in front of you, your body will do what you just imagined it doing. Practice pays off here, too. If you've practiced proper techniques enough before the climb, muscle memory will kick in, and you won't have to think about *how* to do the moves as they come up—you'll just do them.

Thinking Body, Dancing Mind also offers some great ways to overcome fear, which every climber must learn to do. I took a forty-foot ground fall in late 1993, and even though I wasn't hurt physically, the experience brought to the surface fears about falling that I had previously submerged. One way I dealt with them was to accept them and not try to push them aside. I made Fear into a person, giving it eyes, ears, a mouth, and a nose. Instead of letting it debilitate me, I imagined it climbing alongside me, accepting the fact that it would be a part of the climbing experience without letting it stop me.

Mental training must go hand in hand with physical training for the successful athlete. Developing a strong mental attitude isn't easy; it requires work, just like developing strong pecs or abs requires work. An effective training program must include exercises that strengthen the mind as much as the muscles.

– 5 –

Competing

The master boulderer John Gill loved the peace and serenity of bouldering alone, and he was able to do some amazing things solo. But most of us climb better and have more fun in a social setting, and many of us love the excitement and "push" we get from competing against others in bouldering contests.

That doesn't mean you have to run out and enter the next Phoenix Bouldering Contest to have fun. There are lots of competitions around, and if the spur from formal competition doesn't do it for you, you can square off informally against friends.

Bouldering makes great competition. The problems are usually short, so it's pretty easy to get psyched up to try a flash and to find out who can do it. If no one can flash it, see who can do it in the fewest tries.

To test yourself against a range of other boulderers, you might want to enter a formal bouldering competition. Two of the biggest are the Phoenix Bouldering Contest and the Hueco Rocks Rodeo. The PBC, the one I know best, has attracted some five hundred competitors from all over the world. It's traditionally been the big daddy of bouldering contests, and it's a true citizen's race—absolutely anyone can enter.

Held in Oak Flats Campground, between Superior and Globe (actually one hour east of Phoenix), in the middle of the beautiful Arizona desert, the PBC offers something for everyone. There are categories for the good, bad, young, and old, with raffles and plenty of prizes. The area is a huge playground of volcanic rock with many pocketed walls. The rock is dacite, a soft volcanic rock with a hard surface. The contest starts in the morning and lasts for six hours.

At Uniweep Canyon.

Competing in Phoenix

Here are some competition strategies I've learned from my experiences in the PBC. You can adapt them to help you do well in any bouldering competition you enter.

One-finger pockets are prevalent at Phoenix, so I work on them before I arrive. Most competitions have a distinctive feature or features; find out what they are before the contest and prepare for them.

I recommend you preregister as early as possible; big events like Phoenix fill up quickly, especially during the week or two before the contest. It's no fun to be sweating it out on the waiting list. When you get to Phoenix, you'll need to show identification to verify your age. The day before the event, organizers will give you an information packet that includes a map of the area. Look at it right away. Figure out where the sun and shade will be by using the directional symbols. The Arizona desert in April can be scorching; it can also be freezing, when fleece pants are a must. Make sure you prepare for everything. Before the contest, check out weather reports on the Internet so you'll know what to wear.

The map will give you a black-and-white drawing of the entire area, as well as short descriptions of each of the several hundred bouldering sites and canyons. Each bouldering problem is numbered, with assigned points ranging from 1 to 2,000. Take the map back to your tent, vehicle, or motel room and study it carefully, or hold a pow-wow with your climbing mates.

Strategy. Strategy—maybe more than strength—is extremely important in determining the outcome of a bouldering contest. On the map, with a colored pen, highlight the problems you plan to tackle. The problems are spread over a wide area, so you have to plan exactly where you want to go so you don't waste time during the contest. Be prepared, however, to alter your plans if you're forced to by oppressive heat or long lines.

One thing that's bound to change your strategy is discovering which problems are sandbags—those that are harder than they are graded—and which are gimmies—those that are easier than they are graded. All 30-pointers are definitely not created equally. Unfortunately, until you do the problems, there's no way to tell which is which. But if you're on what's rated a 100-pointer and you discover that it's considerably more vicious than the 100-pointer you just tried, you know it's a sandbag and not worth spending energy or time on. The next 100-pointer might be easier. Valuable information about sandbags and gimmies is often floating all around you. Be alert to it. Listen to what other competitors are saying: friends will tell you where the gimmies are; others might let vital information slip. My philosophy is to tell my friends and withhold from my "enemies." If I discover a 500-pointer that's a total gimmie, you can bet that I'm real careful about whom I share the information with.

Long Lines. With five hundred boulderers competing at Phoenix, long lines at the best problems are often a big headache. If you can find out before the competition begins where the most popular spots will be, you can plan to avoid them early in the contest. You don't want to be waiting in line when you could be on the rock racking up points. Trust me on this one. In 1998, Jim Waugh, the main man and Phoenix Bouldering Contest visionary, allowed six hundred climbers to enter because he said the event would never be held again. That year, the lines were enormous, and they really ruined the contest for a lot of people. The evening before the contest, everyone in the advanced and elite categories saw that a large number of big-point problems were at the Tinkerbell Wall, so they decided that was the place to go first. Next morning, Tinkerbell was a madhouse! Then and there, I decided that the best way to proceed was to go first to problems that were not likely to be crowded and get points on my scorecard before I headed to the hot spots.

How to Get Points. On the morning of the event, double-check your supplies: boots, food, water, electrolyte-replacement drink, skin kit, chalk, chalk bag, toothbrush, pens, watch, Clif Bars (or other food). When you arrive at the event, you will pick up your scorecard. Keep it with you all day. If you are serious about competing—don't lose your scorecard.

At Phoenix, you can do as many problems as you like in the six-hour time limit, but only your ten highest scores count. You can attempt any one problem as many times as you like, but I recommend that you move on if you don't complete a problem after three tries, unless you are absolutely positive you can make it on the fourth. Otherwise, you simply waste too much energy on one problem.

Volunteer judges are posted at most stations. If there's no judge around when you complete a problem, you must have a witness initial your scorecard next to the number of the problem you sent. Carry extra pens for this. Witnessing is on the honor system, and although climbers as a whole are an extremely honest group, there are some cheaters out there. Don't cheat on the scorecard—you're really only cheating yourself. Those who get caught cheating are usually humiliated, as well they should be.

The Action. At the crack of the starter's gun, the fun begins. Hundreds of climbers fly off, buzzing around like bees, swarming to the most popular spots. It can be confusing as you try to find the signs that point the way to your chosen starting site. It's also exhilarating. A lot of competitors start out with friends, but they are usually quickly separated. You're soon on your own, and the hectic pace and long lines can sometimes be a little overwhelming. Relax and stay energized. It's a great opportunity to meet people and make new friends.

Some climbers like to start out slowly with some low-rated warm-up problems to work out the kinks and get some quick points on their scorecards. On the more difficult problems, they adapt varying strategies. Some, like Tommy Caldwell, a strong climber in the '95, '96, and '97 contests, go all out on the first try of a problem and stay with it until they send it. Others, like Christian Griffith, a previous winner, listen to their bodies and adapt their strategies accordingly; Christian rarely tries a problem more than three times. Still others, like past winner Timmy Fairfield, believe that the winner is pretty much decided in the first two hours of the contest.

Me, I'm not a morning person. I think I climb better later in the day, even though that's when the weather's the hottest in the Arizona desert. I think the key to success is pacing with a capital P. Keep track of the time—take a watch—during the contest and monitor your rest stops. In Phoenix, you see a lot of climbers race around in the morning, frantically throwing themselves on problem after problem, only to bonk by noon. The best rate seems to be about two or three problems an hour. But it's a cardinal sin not to have your scorecard filled when the final gun sounds. Pick up the pace or try easier problems if you need to; you can always try harder problems once you've logged ten good climbs.

Good pacing means that when you are not climbing or walking to a boulder problem, you are drinking, eating, and resting. Don't forget to have fun either! Carry plenty of water and drink during rests and after every attempt. You should also pound down some calories, although I'm usually so jazzed that I have trouble eating much. For that I invariably pay the price of a pounding headache by day's end.

At any competition, you might find yourself climbing well below your normal level. If that happens, try to maintain a positive attitude. Everyone has an off day. Hang in and complete as many problems as you can—at the very least you'll get a great workout.

Win or not, when the contest is over and you've completed your ten scores, the manzanita scratches and chafed fingers are quickly forgotten. I guarantee that the sense of accomplishment you'll feel will last a lifetime—or at least until it's time to register for the next event.

One more word of wisdom. It really helps to get outside and boulder as much as possible to prepare for the Phoenix contest. Since this event is on real rock, real rock experience is what you need to be successful. The years I did best in Phoenix were the years I trained in Hueco Tanks before the contest. Unfortunately, training in Hueco Tanks is no longer an option—this magical bouldering garden is now closed to climbing. I'm hoping with all my might that someday soon the Texas state parks system will reopen Hueco to climbing. The national non-profit Access Fund, a great organization that promotes responsible climbing, is working diligently to see that this happens. In the meantime, you can train for the PBC in the Buttermilks or, better yet, in the Oak Flats area itself.

– 6 –

Climbing Safely

You usually don't boulder with a rope, so bouldering safely is especially important. Bouldering requires such intense concentration that it's easy for boulderers to forget to stay safe as they focus all their attention on their next move. The number-one rule is for you to take responsibility for you. Even if you have a half dozen spotters, you must be prepared to take charge of your own safety. This chapter looks at how to be safe and avoid injuries on the rock.

Warming Up

I said it before and I'll say it again: before any exercise or climbing session, no matter how short in duration, you must take the time to warm up. More than a few climbers have gotten injured because they skipped the warm-up or didn't take warming up seriously. I warm up my large muscle groups—back, biceps, chest, quads—first and then move to the smaller ones and the tendons, ligaments, and so forth. I climb on big, easy holds first; after my large muscles are warm, I climb on smaller holds.

During the climbing session, I work on staying warm and loose as well. During breaks I always stretch my fingers and forearms and massage any areas that feel pumped or sore and shake my arms out to get rid of the pump. I also drink a lot of water during the warm-up phase and while I am resting and depumping.

Next during warm-up, I change angles up the rock to warm all my muscles from all directions. I do short, easy movements until I feel loose and powerful. Then I do one a little harder, ideally one I've done before and wired. This lets me know if I'm sufficiently warm.

The final stage of my on-the-rock warm-up is to do a boulder problem I know well and can barely deal with, which forces me to warm up each and every muscle the problem demands. I might do the first two moves, then return to the ground. Then I repeat the first two moves while someone supports my weight, then continue on without help to the next two moves before returning to the ground. If you are preparing to attempt a particular problem, it's a good idea to warm up on all the different moves before going for the linkage.

After my warm-up, which usually takes about thirty minutes (longer if I've had multiple rest days), I take a quick water break, getting my mind and body ready for what's ahead. Breaks are important. Don't throw yourself at boulder problems all day long without taking breaks. You'll perform better if you relax and calm yourself, and rehydrate, between problems or attempts. Make sure your muscles are restored before you tackle a difficult circuit. This will help you avoid the dreaded "flash pump"—total muscle fatigue brought on by going too hard too quickly. Warming up properly will make your workout more productive and prolong your climbing day.

After I've warmed up, I stretch, as described in Chapter 4, always remembering to stretch my fingers and hands. I feel the stretch, enjoying the low-level discomfort, but I quickly back off from any pain. I always work both sides of my body.

Landing Safely

If you're up on a boulder problem that's ten feet high, you're actually free soloing. It's just as serious. When I'm up that high, I'm always thinking *Where do I plan to land? How safe is the landing? Is there a clear path to the ground? Is there an ankle-breaking root down there?*

Use a crash pad when you boulder. The least a pad does is prevent a lot of wear and tear on the body. The most it can do is save you from serious injury. Pads are especially valuable when you're recovering from knee or ankle injuries, but I usually use one even when I'm healthy to help me stay that way. Using a crash pad will also let you feel comfortable enough to go for it with a vengeance.

I really like the Cordless, Metolious, and Pad Industries crash pads. They have models that are four to five inches thick and roll up into backpacks. I use them to carry water, food, chalk, shoes, and other gear. There are plenty of other brands to choose from; shop around.

Bouldering up high is really free soloing.

It's pretty easy to make your own pad by folding a couple of Enso-lite pads—usually available at outdoor shops—in half and wrapping them in duct tape. Tape carpet wedges on both sides; make sure they're well attached and that some carpet is exposed so that you can wipe off your feet before starting a problem. Attach a strap for carrying. Or use an old mattress for climbing indoors—just make sure there are no springs poking out.

Some climbing gyms use strips of tire rubber for a landing site; take note if there's tire wire sticking out of these.

Learn how to land properly even if you use a crash pad. Keep your knees and hips bent and sag into the landing so you don't jar your joints on impact. Practice landing indoors on a good pad.

Spotting

Just as climbers must take responsibility for their own safety, spotters must concentrate on keeping the climber safe to the exclusion of all else. They must not be distracted by a hawk screaming in the air above them or a sexy climber pulling up on a nearby ledge—or by their own anger if the climber they're spotting just outdid them. (They can use that anger to their advantage when they're back on the rock.) Refer to Chapter 3 for more tips on proper spotting.

Crash pads make bouldering more comfortable.

Skin Care

Bouldering can be murder on the hands, especially the fingers and palms. Anyone who does any bouldering at all will quickly become acquainted with the bloody flapper, and although loose skin seems tame compared to a shattered bone or a ripped ligament, it can be painful enough to end your day of climbing. That's why you must be prepared. Carry a skin kit that includes these items:

- Nail clippers
- Medium-grade sandpaper
- Tincture of benzoin compound or Tough Skin spray
- Athletic tape
- Vitamin E oil
- Aloe vera gel
- Neosporin

Here's how a skin kit can save the day, from personal experience. In Hueco Tanks, while attempting a boulder problem called Brand New Religion V7, I slipped on a hold and tore a dime-size flap of skin off my middle finger. Major bummer. But I was prepared. First, I clipped off the remaining flaps of skin. Then I gently sanded the rough spots with medium-grade sandpaper until they were nice and smooth. (If the skin is too tender, you might not be able to do this.) I sprayed on Tough Skin, which stung like hell (this stuff is actually an antiseptic; it was once used for surgery to stick both sides of incisions together before stitch up). Then I backtaped the injury so that the sticky side of the tape didn't touch the wound itself. It wasn't pretty, and I wasn't pain free, but I could get back on the rock within a matter of minutes.

Neosporin is a good way to treat a bad flapper before taping it. It will help cut the pain and help it heal more quickly. If the skin is thin and close to bleeding, apply vitamin E oil and aloe vera gel to help it heal.

I occasionally use ibuprofen during hard bouldering when my fingertips start screaming with pain even though the skin is intact—but only when I feel I really need to and my body is injury free. I've used it at the Phoenix Bouldering Contest, when long hours of intense bouldering on supersharp rock made my fingertips bawl. Four hundred milligrams of ibuprofen will make my fingertips numb—so numb, in fact, that I make a point of regularly checking them for flappers I can't feel. Please remember that ibuprofen can have side effects: be careful and consult your doctor before using it to help you climb.

Injuries

I'm not a doctor, but I've had my share of injuries, so I think I can pass on some helpful information about avoiding injuries and dealing with them if they happen. Because we tend to do the same moves over and over, the most common types of injuries boulderers suffer from are overuse injuries. It's important to avoid wearing out specific muscles needed on a particular problem by trying it all day. Switch to a different problem; when you've recovered, you can return to the first one.

The intense concentration bouldering requires makes it easy for boulderers to forget that they're putting their bodies through all kinds of contortions. The challenge is to give one hundred percent to the moves while at the same time staying alert to the possibility of injury.

One particular overuse injury seems to plague boulderers—pulling the tendon that wraps around the ring finger between the second and third joints. A severe pull of this tendon, or any other tendon in the fingers, will cause pain to radiate through the wrist and into the forearm. Not fun, but you will recover. Pulled tendons in the elbow are also pretty common.

If you feel a sharp pain in the finger or elbow (or anywhere else, for that matter)—the tell-tale sign of a tendon pull—stop climbing immediately. Take anti-inflammatories and, most importantly, apply ice to the injured area as soon as possible—which is the key to lessening the severity and decreasing the recovery time from acute injuries such as tendon pulls and muscle strains. Ice the injury immediately even if you plan to go to the doctor. Besides relieving pain, ice slows blood flow and reduces internal bleeding and swelling. This helps limit tissue damage and speeds up the healing process.

Here are some general tips for icing: Commercial freezable packs work fine, but plain ol' ice is just as effective. Put cubes or crushed ice in a heavy plastic bag, use bags of frozen veggies, or freeze a wet towel and wrap it around the injured area. Or soak the area in a bowl of half water and half ice. Apply the ice to the injury for ten to twenty minutes, rest without ice for two hours, then repeat the cycle during your waking hours for the next two days. Do not ice for more than twenty minutes at a time or you might damage skin and nerves with the cold.

The first twinge of even slight pain you feel when exercising may be the first warning sign of an overuse injury, such as tendonitis. Apply ice to tender areas as soon as you can, even if you managed to finish your climb. Reapply it several times a day for the next two days. If the tender area starts to swell, which is likely with acute injuries, use ice as part of a self-treatment plan athletes know as RICE, which means:

- **R**est the injured body part.
- Apply **I**ce.
- Apply **C**ompression.
- **E**levate the injury above the heart.

Resting is an important part of the treatment. It reduces pain and keeps the injury from being aggravated. Compression and elevation prevent fluids from pooling in the tissues. The best way to compress an injury is to wrap a towel or an Ace-type bandage around it. Compress and ice at the same time by holding the ice bag in place with the bandage. Don't compress so tightly that you restrict circulation.

An acute injury shouldn't be treated with heat for at least forty-eight hours after the injury occurs. In the past, athletes applied heat right after icing; some still do. But the heat actually stimulates blood flow and works to increase swelling. Most sports doctors and trainers recommend sticking with ice for at least the first two days. When the swelling goes down, you can then try either damp or dry heat.

Torn knee cartilage, either the medial meniscus (inside) or the anterior meniscus (outside), is another common bouldering injury. High stepping, heel-hooking, and the drop-knee are the main culprits. The tear can often make a sickeningly loud crack, almost like a gunshot.

Boulderers are also susceptible to ankle sprains or breaks. My first-aid kit, which I always take with me when I climb outdoors, comes complete with athletic tape, which is the first-line treatment for ankle injuries. Atwater Carey makes a great backcountry first-aid kit.

My first-aid kit came in handy one afternoon several years ago in Hueco Tanks, when my friend Steven Schneider fell off a high boulder problem and broke his ankle. He went into minor shock, so we had to keep him comfortable and calm. We found pieces of wood and used tape from the kit to fashion a splint. Then three of us trudged a mile and a half back to the car, carrying Steven and our crash pads. We must have looked like shell-shocked soldiers returning from battle.

Remember: if you are trying a move that causes pain, stop immediately and go on to something else. Completing a problem isn't worth the risk of an injury that might sideline you for days, weeks, or even years.

Recovery

Drinking lots of water is an essential part of the recovery process, whether you are recovering from an injury or just resting between climbing days; fluid replacement is as important to recovering muscles as it is to working muscles. Not only that, but water is a key to good overall health, and I'm convinced it slows down the aging process.

Specific over-the-counter remedies are also a part of my recovery process. I use arnica gel (brand name Arniflora) to treat bumps, bruises, and overuse injuries. It comes in spray or gel-cream that you can apply directly to the inflamed area. I always carry arnica with me; I rub it on my stiff hands and fingers at the end of a climbing session. It offers immediate relief. Sublingual arnica Montana is the pill form. For sprains, bruises, muscle soreness, and tendonitis, I recommend a home-opathic remedy called ruta graveolens.

Standard anti-inflammatories such as aspirin or ibuprofen work well to treat overuse injuries. Acetaminophen (usually Tylenol) will relieve muscle soreness, but it's not an anti-inflammatory. Trainers and doctors can recommend stronger medications that include cortisone and its derivatives to eliminate pain and swelling very quickly, but these drugs—which usually require a prescription—can produce serious side effects. They also can mask the pain that serves as a warning sign that you are doing damage to your body, allowing you to keep on exercising, perhaps causing permanent damage to an injured tissue. Use these drugs only under medical supervision and for brief periods of time.

I've found that a deep-tissue massage, which stretches and loosens my muscles big time, is, on occassion, a worthwhile part of my recovery process. It's expensive, but worth it: I've done some of my best bouldering on the second day after a massage. (You're usually so relaxed that you're pretty useless on the rock immediately after a massage, however.) I also sometimes go to a chiropractor for quick and simple adjustments to my spine, fingers, wrists, knees, ankles, and toes.

When you return to climbing after resting an injury, don't work the affected area so much that pain returns. Go slow—return to your usual workout routine gradually. Stop immediately if the pain returns and don't continue. You should be free of pain before, during, and after the activity when you return to your usual level of exercise.

Identifying exactly what caused your injury is an important but often overlooked part of the recovery process. Was it poor equipment? Poor technique? Some other factor? Find out and correct the problem.

Resist the temptation to rest longer than two days after an injury unless it is really severe. Resting longer than that will start to weaken your muscles and stiffen your joints. If you don't keep healing tissue moving, it repairs itself with irregular scar tissue, like a scab; exercising during healing promotes straighter, stronger scars.

It's important to maintain your aerobic fitness as you recover from injury. Bike or swim if you can't run or climb. If you're into weight training, do more reps with less weight. When you start climbing after an injury, work the injured area very slowly, building up gradually to a full range of motion.

Retreating

The safest way to proceed on the rock is sometimes to retreat. I've climbed more than my fair share of boulder problems from which I had to be rescued when I should have retreated before I got into trouble. It's maddening and embarrassing and I don't plan on letting it happen again, but that's what can happen if you don't pay enough attention to your intended escape route before you get up high.

When I was living in Bishop, California, bouldering in the Buttermilks and Deadman's Summit near Mammoth Lakes, I once climbed Grandma Peabody Boulder and felt a wave of joy when I made it to the top. My happiness quickly turned to fear, however, when I couldn't find a safe way off. I tried everything—down-climbing, jumping off; nothing worked, and the sun was beginning to set in a major way. The thought of having to spend the night up there made me panic. I began yelling for help, with little hope that anyone would hear me. After about twenty very scary minutes, a man appeared from nowhere and helped me down-climb to safety. (Even though my savior was Dale Bard, and his rescue was the start of a long friendship that endures today, I wouldn't want to go through that experience again for anything.) Learn from my mistake: When you are bouldering high off the deck, always look for holds that will help you down. Try to find the line of least resistance. Know how you will descend before you ever reach the top.

Accidents

It's an unfortunate truth that if you climb long enough, you or someone else in your party is bound to have an accident. If you're lucky, it will be minor. But there's always a chance it will be serious. Accidents can happen to anyone, not just the inexperienced or "other climbers."

Even the most careful and skilled climbers can find themselves in dangerous predicaments. Being prepared with the knowledge and ability to do what needs to be done if an accident happens is the best way to avoid a disaster.

I'll offer some brief guidelines here on dealing with accidents, but the best way to prepare yourself is to read a book that covers the subject in detail or, better still, take a first-aid course from an expert.

When an Accident Happens

- If the victim is unconscious, make sure air passages are not blocked. Try to keep the patient on his side or stomach.
- Make certain the victim can't fall or injure himself further. He may start moving when he regains consciousness.
- Stop any bleeding using pressure with a clean handkerchief or first-aid dressing. Cover open wounds with clean, light dressing.
- Make the injured person as comfortable as possible. Keep him warm and dry, but move him as little as necessary. *If you suspect a spinal injury, do not move the patient at all.*
- Use a temporary splint if a limb is broken.
- Hot drinks are good to warm up the victim, but don't give him anything to eat or drink if you suspect internal injuries. Warm up the victim gradually is he's suffering from exposure.
- If you need to attract help, yell, blow a whistle, flash a flashlight or mirror, or send up a flare. Remember the recognized Alpine Distress Signal—six long blasts or flashes repeated every sixty seconds.

Climbing can be risky, but preparation and common sense reduce the risk substantially. When you're climbing, listen to and trust your inner voice. Don't hesitate to back off or retreat if you think it's the best thing to do. It might just save your life.

− 7 −

Ethics

There are several ethical questions all good boulderers should think about. Some are clear ethical transgressions; others, depending on your point of view, may or may not be violations.

Cheater Stones

Cheater stones are rocks piled on the ground that allow a climber to reach the first hold of a problem. I don't have a problem with cheater stones, but some of my peers, most notably John Sherman, certainly do. To them, using cheater stones is, well, cheating. To my mind, however, using cheater stones is valid if, for example, the first hold of a problem is seven feet off the ground, within reach of taller climbers but beyond the grasp of those of us who are five-foot-four, or shorter. I mean, why should a killer boulder problem be available to only the tall? Some would say that each and every climber shouldn't be able to do each and every climb. Why not just accept that there are some climbs that some people will never be able to do? they ask. I can see their point, but I don't agree with it. If using cheater stones makes you happy, then I say they're awesome. After all, we only have one life to live—why not live it to its fullest?

Cheater stone can really help you on a problem that has a strenuous sit-down start. You might do the first couple of moves of the problem, descend, and then use a cheater stone to cut out the strenuous beginning and work on the upper part of the problem. After you fire the upper section, you can link the two parts.

Truth of Ascent

My thinking on cheater stones certainly doesn't mean that I advocate any
kind of dishonesty about what you've accomplished. The key is truth of
ascent. Climbers should never kid themselves or sugarcoat their climbs
by calling them something other than what they were. A red-point is a
red-point, a top rope is a top rope, so call them as they are.

Tick Marks

Tick marks are the traces of chalk left by past climbers that create a road
map of routes and holds on many boulder problems. Lots of climbers
hate tick marks even though using chalk is for the most part universally
accepted in climbing. They think they make solving a problem too easy.
Plus, they're unsightly.

 I must confess—I use tick marks. In fact, when my friends or even
my enemies see a boulder problem I'm working on, with my giant
chalk boxes drawn around the holds, they think I must be blind. But I
do erase the marks after I send the problem, using a toothbrush if I have
to. For the good of the sport, you should do the same. You should also
avoid colored chalk; it can stain the rock. Use only white. And don't use
Pouf like they do in France; it can make the rock greasy.

Tick mark.

Chipping

To me, chipping is completely unacceptable ninety-nine percent of the time. Chipping means using a chisel or other tool to make a small hold bigger or deeper or a file to make a hold more comfortable by eliminating sharp edges. Chipping is a slap in the face of nature and your fellow climbers, creating ugliness where beauty once reigned.

Nothing makes me sadder than returning to a beloved boulder problem only to discover that holds have been altered to make the route user-friendlier. This has happened to me more than once—at Hueco Tanks, where a number of boulder problems have been chipped, and elsewhere. I really don't understand how anyone could defend the rights of maverick climbers to artificially reduce the rock to their level. What about the rights of climbers who can handle, or are at least challenged by, the original degree of difficulty? I say leave the rock as it is, and return to it later when you're able to challenge it on its own terms. If you succeed then, you'll know you really accomplished something. If that day never comes, then at least you will have allowed future generations to take their shot.

There might be some very few instances (one percent) when chipping is okay. Maybe if the rock at a potential bouldering area is unacceptably loose and chossy and chipping away the loose, ugly rock makes it a decent climb. Maybe.

Bottom line: the call is yours. But be prepared to suffer the consequences if you chip. Most climbers consider it a big no-no.

Top Roping

Top roping is both an ethical issue and a safety issue. There are certain times I have top roped a problem out of fear for my orthopedic health. The rope may protect me for only four or five moves, but that can be enough to ensure safety and prevent an injury. In 1990, I had an operation to repair torn cartilage in my knee, and I don't want to go through that again. I know that purists would give me grief about top roping, but I believe that as long as we're honest about our means of ascent, it's strictly a personal matter.

Touchy Feely

When a spotter touches you while you are on the rock, it's a problem, an ethical violation I call "touchy feely." No matter how tiny, insignificant, even accidental the touch seems, it's still technically cheating. Yet

I see touchy feelies all the time. At Hueco Tanks, it sometimes looks as if climbers are being pushed up boulder problems. At the end of the day, these same climbers sit around the campfire and brag about all the problems they sent.

Sometimes the touch is accidental. The climber tries a difficult move and her feet swing out and just brush the spotter. It doesn't seem as though the touch affected the move at all. But it might have—maybe it stopped the climber's momentum and helped her stay on the rock. It's tough to say. Should the touch keep the climber from honestly claiming the ascent?

In 1994, Frederick Nicole came to Yosemite from Switzerland to do the first ascent of the Dominator. He cruised the first part, an overhanging roof that's also the crux. Near the top, during a lunge move, his feet released from the rock and hit somebody. He continued to the top, and believed he had made a legitimate ascent. But others had questions: What if that person wasn't there? What if the contact stopped

Nicole from flying off completely? Did he have enough body tension to swing his feet back and finish the problem, or would he have fallen? No one knows for sure.

Weight off is a legitimate training technique.

On Slice of Life, Rifle.

I personally think that Fred is the man when it comes to bouldering and that the Dominator was his for sure. Valley locals agree. But the situation does raise difficult questions, and it will probably always lead to heated discussions about the ethics of touchy feelies. It's easy to see why some top-flight boulderers refuse to use spotters so they don't risk disqualification for an accidental tap.

I think that the one time the touchy feely is acceptable is when the climber is working a problem that is way too difficult for their current skill level. The little bit of support a spotter can offer might take enough body weight off the climber so they can do a move they couldn't do a hundred percent by themselves. Doing the move with a bit of help lets them recruit the specific muscle fibers needed and deposit the move in their muscle memory so they will eventually be able to go it alone. This is a legitimate practice technique I call "weight off."

Trash

I've found in my travels that most bouldering sites are absolutely gorgeous—not only because of the routes they offer (which make my heart pound with excitement) but also because of the surrounding countryside, whether it's rugged mountains or leafy green woodlands. It's up to the boulderers who climb at these sites to keep them as beautiful as they are. If you slow down and enjoy your surroundings—one of the best parts of bouldering anyway—it will soon become second nature to clean up your own mess *and* the messes others leave behind.

Glossary

anchor: the point at which a fixed rope, a rappel rope, or a belay is secured to rock, snow, or ice by any of various means.

artificial climbing wall: a climbing surface—often indoors, made of board, stone, or a polyester resin and sand mixture—that has a variety of manufactured holds attached.

balance climbing: a technique for climbing smooth rock in which the climber uses handholds and footholds that allow her to stay balanced.

belay: to tend the climbing rope, ready to immediately put enough friction on the rope to arrest a climber's fall. Friction is caused by the rope passing around the belayer's body or through a belay device. A universal safety practice, the belay also refers to the whole system set up to make belaying possible, including the anchor that holds the belayer in place.

belay device: metal piece of equipment that forces a bend in the climbing rope to create enough friction to prevent the rope's movement in case of a fall. *See also* descender and figure-eight.

big wall: a steep, vertical rock face 1,000 feet or more from bottom to top.

biner: (pronounced "beaner"), slang for carabiner.

body belay: *see* waist belay.

bolt: a metal rod hammered into a pre-drilled hole in the rock to serve as a multidirectional anchor. Bolting remains a controversial practice.

bolted route: a route entirely protected by bolts.

bombproof: a hold or belay that is considered completely safe, regardless of how much force is put on it.

boulder problem: a route up a boulder, usually named and rated.

bridging (stemming): a technique in which the climber pushes out to the sides with hands and/or feet. Often used to climb chimneys or dihedrals.

bucket: a large bombproof hold.

bulge: a small overhang.

bumblies: novice climbers who have no idea what they are doing.

carabiner: an oval or D-shaped metal snap-link device used for attaching a climbing rope to anchors.

chalk: light magnesium carbonate used by climbers to keep their hands dry and thus improve handholds.

chalk bag: a bag worn at a climber's waist that holds powdered chalk.

chickenhead: protruding knob on a rock face; makes a good hold.

chimney: a crack in the rock wide enough so that a climber can squeeze his whole body into it.

chimneying: climbing a chimney by pressing against the sides with the feet and the back.

chock: Originally a rock, then a machine nut, now a metal device that's wedged in a crack or behind a flake, around which a runner can be threaded and then clipped to a rope for an anchor point. The two basic chocks are *wedges* and *hexes*. Also called a chockstone.

chop: to remove someone else's protection, especially bolts, from the rock.

clean climbing: a way of climbing that leaves the rock unscarred and unblemished after the climbing team passes.

corner: an outside junction of two planes of rock, approximately at right angles. (Contrasted with dihedral.)

crack: a gap or fracture in the rock; cracks can be thin seams or wide chimneys.

crag: a low cliff that's one or two pitches high.

crimping: gripping small holds on the rock by keeping the fingers together and bending them at the first knuckle.

crux: the most difficult part or parts of a pitch or climb.

dihedral: a high-angled inside corner where two rock planes intersect.

direct: the most direct way up a route, usually steeper and thus more difficult than ordinary routes.

double dyno: two dynos in succession, or a dynamic move where both hands and both feet come off the rock.

dyno: a dynamic movement for gaining a hold just beyond the climber's reach in which one hand and both feet come off the rock.

edging: using the sides of climbing boots to stand on thin ledges.

exposed: a steep, difficult route with a lot of air between it and the ground.

exposure: a long drop beneath a climber's feet.

face: a rock wall that's steeper than 60 degrees.

face climbing: using handholds and footholds on an open rock face.

finger crack: a crack in the rock so thin that a climber can fit only one finger into it.

first ascent: the first time a route has been climbed.

fist crack: a crack the size of a fist.

fist jam: a hold in which the climber shoves his hand into a fist crack and than makes a fist to create an anchor point. (Pushing the thumb into the palm creates a larger fist.)

flake: a thin, partly detached leaf of rock. Also, preparing a rope so that it doesn't get tangled on the rock.

flapper: a torn flap of skin on the hand.

flaring crack: a crack with sides that flare out.

flash: to climb a route on the very first try without falling or using a top rope.

free climbing: climbing using only natural handholds and footholds—hardware is used only for protection and not for support. (Contrasted with aid climbing.)

friction climbing: to climb using only the friction created between shoes and rock or hands and rock instead of distinct holds.

Gaston: a move where the climber grabs a vertical hold and pushes it away in the direction of the next hold.

glacial erratic: a boulder deposited by a glacier far from its original source.

glacial groove: a deep scratch on a rock surface caused by the movement of sediment-laden glaciers over bedrock.

glacis: an easy-angled slab of rock that's between horizontal and 30 degrees.

gripped: a climber who's terrified about climbing higher or further.

groove: a shallow, vertical crack.

gully: steep-sided chasm that's deep enough to walk inside.

hand traverse: moving across the face of the rock supported mainly by the hands.

headwall: the sheerest, often most difficult, section of a cliff or mountain, usually its uppermost.

hold: a feature on the rock face that a climber can grip with the hands or stand on.

horn: a protruding rock over which a sling can be hung for an anchor.

jam crack: a gap in the rock that a climber can shove his fingers, hand, fist, or feet into to create an anchor point.

jamming: wedging fingers, hand, fist, or feet into a jam crack.

jug: a large, indented hold that's easy to grip.

kernmantle: standard climbing rope in which the interior *kern*, made up of one or more braided units, is protected by an outer braided sheath, or *mantle*.

laybacking: a way of climbing aretes, corners with cracks, and cracks offset in walls in which you grab a vertical edge, pull with the hands, and push with the feet then walk them up almost alongside the hands.

ledge: a flat area on a cliff or mountain.

lock-off: a technique that gets you ready for the next move in which you pull up hard on a horizontal hold, getting your hand to shoulder level.

manteling: pushing down on a ledge with both hands until the body is supported on stiffened arms, then moving a foot up to replace one hand, then standing on the ledge.

natural line: a climb that follows an obvious crack or gully up the face of a cliff.

niche: a small pit in a rock face that's usually large enough to hold a climber.

nose: a broad, jutting protrusion of rock.

off-finger crack: a crack too wide to finger jam, but too narrow to hand jam.

off-hand jam: a crack too wide to hand jam, but too narrow to fist jam.

off-width: a crack too wide to fist jam, but too narrow to fit the whole body into.

on-sight: to climb a route with no previous knowledge of the necessary moves.

on-sight flash: to climb a route on the first try without falling and with no previous knowledge of its moves.

open book: a high-angled inside rock corner, a dihedral.

overhang: rock that exceeds 90 degrees.

overuse injury: tissue damage caused by doing too much too fast (in contrast to traumatic injury).

palming: holding the hand flat against the rock to create friction between the palm and the climbing surface.

pedestal: a flat-topped pinnacle detached from other features.

pinnacle: a partially detached feature, like a church steeple.

pocket: a shallow hole in the surface of the rock.

pressure hold: pressing sideways and downward on a handhold or foothold to maintain your position.

put up: to make the first ascent of a route.

rating systems: terms or numbers used to describe the difficulty of climbs; there are seven major rating systems.

redpoint: linkage of a route from beginning to end without coming off the rock.

rock-climbing boots: soft boots with flat rubber soles that grip the rock; there are dozens of brands and styles.

roof: an overhanging, horizontal section of rock.

route: one way up a cliff; there mights be dozens with different names and ratings.

sandbag: a climb that's more difficult than its rating would indicate.

scoop: a pit in the rock face that's shallower than a niche.

scramble: an easy climb that doesn't require a rope.

scree: a slope that's covered with loose stones.

seam: a crack too thin for fingers but wide enough to accept small chocks or copperheads.

second generation: a quick double move with the same hand.

sewing-machine leg: violent shaking in the leg resulting from holding a bent-knee position too long.

slab: large, smooth rock face inclined between 30 and 60 degrees.

smearing: putting as much of the sole of the foot on the rock as possible, using friction to gain a hold.

soloing: climbing alone, roped or unroped, aided or free.

spotting: assisting a climber by standing below them, ready to catch them or prevent injury if they fall.

static move: a climbing move in which at least two points of contact (e.g., a hand and a foot)

remain in contact with the rock (in contrast to dyno).

stemming: *see* bridging.

talus: rock fragments at the base of a slope.

toe-hooking: gripping an edge with the toe or toes.

top rope: (TR) a rope anchored above you for security during a more difficult climb, or using a rope anchored above you to climb a pitch.

touchy-feely: when the spotter makes contact with the climber, an ethical consideration.

traverse: to move across the face of the rock instead of straight up.

tunnel vision: focus on only a small area of rock directly in front of the climber, often causing beginners to ignore good holds off to the side.

undercling: a hold gripped from below with the palms up.

wall: a steep cliff that's between 60 and 90 degrees.

Sponsorship

A sponsor's relationship with a well-known athlete is quite simple: The sponsor pays the athlete to train, and in exchange, the sponsor has the right to use the athlete's image in advertisements, posters, and other publicity. The athlete may also be asked to appear at trade shows or other sales events.

If you're ready to become a professional climber, you can contact various corporations to apply for sponsorship. The following corporations sponsor Bobbi Bensman.